VOLUME 2   BASIC BIOLOGY IN COLOR SERIES

The PLANT WORLD

By PROF. JEAN VALLIN

Lycée Henri Poincaré, Nancy, France

Edited by CHARLES D. HEATH, M.A.
White Plains High School, White Plains, N.Y.

Scientific Adviser E. J. CONNELL

MAPLE

STERLING
PUBLISHING CO., INC.
NEW YORK

Oak Tree Press
London and Sydney

NOTE

The taxonomy, or classification, used in this book is that of "Gray's Manual of Botany," 8th edition, re-written and expanded by M. L. Fernald.

Translated by L. F. Wise and adapted by
Charles D. Heath and E. J. Connell

Revised Edition

Copyright © 1969, 1967 by
Sterling Publishing Co., Inc.
419 Park Avenue South, New York, N.Y. 10016
British edition published in Great Britain and the Commonwealth
by Oak Tree Press, Ltd., 116 Baker St., London W1
Original French editions published by Bordas, Editeur, Paris,
from the Collection Charles Désiré
under various titles © 1959, 1960, 1962, 1963
Manufactured in the United States of America
Library of Congress Catalog Card No.: 67–16012
Standard Book Number 8069–3552 –9
UK 7061 1132 9   8069–3553 –7

CONTENTS

Yew

THE BEAN 5

THE TULIP 13

THE BUTTERCUP 17

THE MAPLE 20

THE CHERRY 24

THE POTATO 29

THE OAK 32

THE CARROT 36

THE DANDELION 40

WHEAT 45

THE ARUM 50

THE PINE 54

POLLINATION 60

DISPERSAL OF FRUITS AND SEEDS 68

VEGETATIVE PROPAGATION 74

FERNS 78

MOSSES 83

SIMPLE FLOWERLESS PLANTS 89

THE MUSHROOM — A FUNGUS 94

LICHENS 101

CLASSIFICATION OF THE PLANTS STUDIED 105

FLORAL DIAGRAMS 106

GLOSSARY-INDEX 107

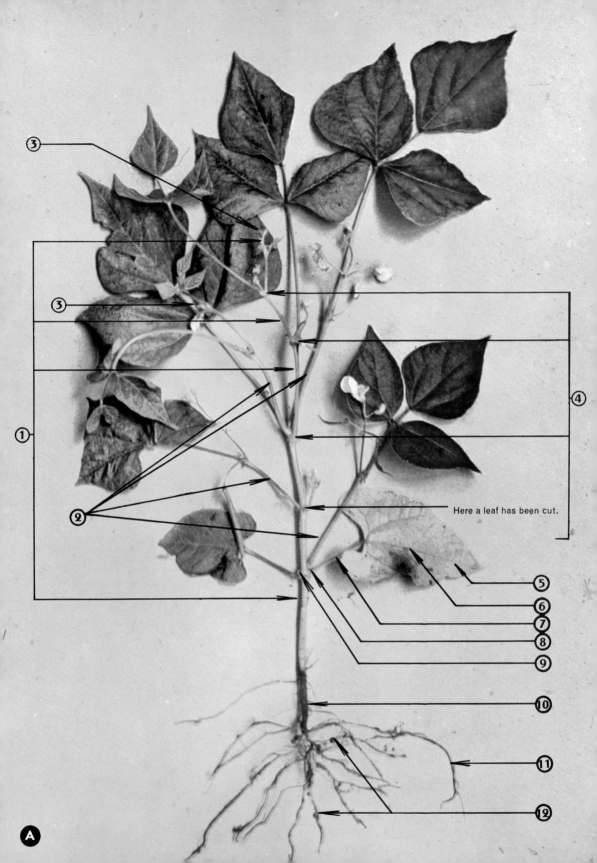

Here a leaf has been cut.

A

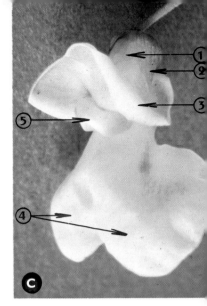

× 2/3   3 ×

THE BEAN

STRUCTURE OF A FLOWERING PLANT

The bean is a food plant, well known because of its fruits and seeds. A study of its structure will help you to understand the meaning of many terms used in the following chapters.

VEGETATIVE SYSTEM

Study a French or haricot bean plant (*Phaseolus vulgaris*) that has been carefully dug up (photo A). You will see that it consists of an aerial part and an underground part, which together constitute the vegetative system.

THE AERIAL PART: You can distinguish a cylindrical axis, the principal stem (1), from which secondary stems or branches grow (2). Because this stem is green and supple, it is said to be herbaceous. At the end of each stem, you can see a small swollen structure: this is called a terminal bud (3).

The stem and the branches bear green, blade-shaped organs called leaves. The areas where these leaves join the stems are called nodes (4) and the space between two nodes is an internode.

Look at the two leaves on each side of the base of the main stem: they are said to be opposed. The leaves of the other nodes, being solitary, are said to be isolated in an alternate arrangement.

Each leaf consists of: a flat part, called the blade (5) permeated by veins (6); a narrow part, the petiole (7); and a widened out base, the sheath (8).

The two opposed leaves, which have a one-piece blade, are simple leaves. All the other leaves, whose blades are composed of three small parts called leaflets are compound leaves. Within the axil of the leaves are small buds called the axillary buds (9).

THE UNDERGROUND PART: The stem continues into the soil through a brown organ which tapers; this is the main root (10). It divides into numerous secondary roots (11), which themselves subdivide. On the roots are small swellings called nodules (12).

The Flower

The flowers, or the resulting fruits, are grouped on small axes situated on the stems. Such groupings are inflorescences (photo B),

5

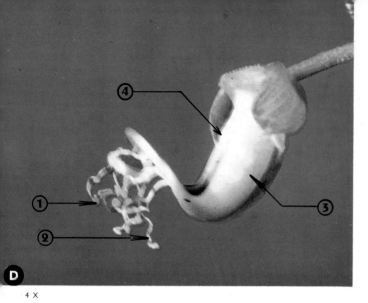

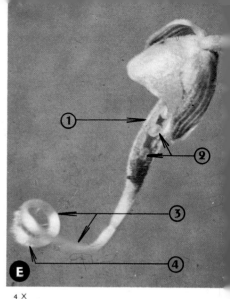

D 4 X

E 4 X

1 X

F

and each consists of a principal axis (peduncle) from which run lateral axes ending in a flower (raceme).

Consider an isolated flower (photo C). The axis carrying it is the pedicel. The floral parts are joined to the swollen end of this, the receptacle. To study this flower, detach the different floral pieces, one by one, with forceps or tweezers. This operation (photos C, D, E), which you can perform more easily on a sweet pea flower, will show you that the flower of a bean or pea consists of:

● 5 small, yellowish parts, the sepals (photo C, 1). These are joined to one another and to the receptacle. This assembly, resembling a cup, is called the calyx. Here the calyx is flanked by two small leaves called bracts (C, 2).

● 5 parts, more or less colored, the petals, which alternate with the sepals. This assembly forms the corolla. The petals can be pulled out separately: they are free. Furthermore, as they differ in shape and size, the corolla is irregular and because this corolla, from a distance, resembles a butterfly, it is said to be a papilion-aceous corolla. The large erect petal is called the standard (C, 3), the two lateral petals, wings (C, 4), and the assembly of two lower petals joined by their end, the keel (5). In the bean, the keel is coiled up, but in the sweet pea

6

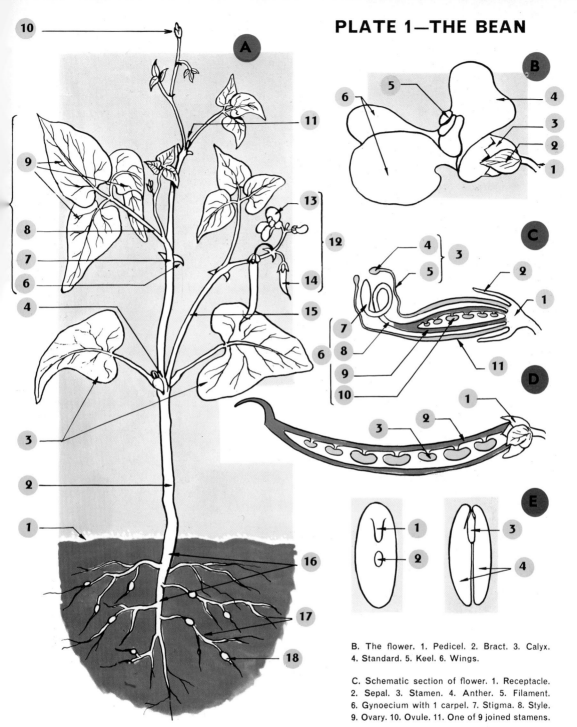

PLATE 1—THE BEAN

A. The whole plant. 1. Soil. 2. Main stem. 3. Simple opposite leaves. 4. Node. 5. Compound leaf. 6. Stipule. 7. Sheath. 8. Petiole. 9. Compound leaf. 10. Terminal bud. 11. Axillary bud. 12. Inflorescence. 13. Flower. 14. Fruit. 15. Secondary stem. 16. Main root. 17. Secondary root. 18. Nodule.

B. The flower. 1. Pedicel. 2. Bract. 3. Calyx. 4. Standard. 5. Keel. 6. Wings.

C. Schematic section of flower. 1. Receptacle. 2. Sepal. 3. Stamen. 4. Anther. 5. Filament. 6. Gynoecium with 1 carpel. 7. Stigma. 8. Style. 9. Ovary. 10. Ovule. 11. One of 9 joined stamens.

D. The fruit (pod). 1. Persistent calyx. 2. Pericarp. 3. Seed.

E. Seed viewed from its concave side and seed with testa removed. 1. Swelling of radicle. 2. Hilum. 3. Radicle. 4. Cotyledons.

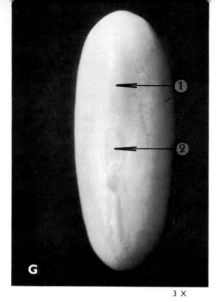

G

3 X

its shape is like the keel of a ship, hence its name.

● 10 parts (photo D) called stamens, the assembly of which forms the androecium. Each stamen consists of a slender filament (2), which supports a swollen organ, the anther (1), from which a yellow powder, pollen, escapes. Here 9 stamens are partly joined by their filament (3), and one remains free (4).

● A green organ (photo E), composed of a single part, the pistil, which constitutes the gynoecium. This pistil consists of:

● A long, swollen part, the ovary (1), which has been cut lengthwise to show the ovules (2) contained inside it. Since this ovary is above the other floral parts, it is a superior ovary.

● A narrow part, coiled into a spiral, the style (3). Its end, hairy and sticky, is the stigma (4).

The flower of the bean, having at one and the same time a calyx, a corolla, an androecium, and a gynoecium, is a complete flower.

This flower, although irregular, can be cut into halves, each of which is the mirror image of the other; it has a bilateral symmetry.

The composition of any flower can be summarized either by a drawing called a floral diagram (see page 106) or by a floral formula. In either case the assemblies of the calyx, corolla, androecium, and gynoecium must be given.

Fruit

When the fruit is young, it is green, fleshy, and edible. In photo F, it has been opened to show its contents, the seeds in formation. At its base is the calyx (1), which is indeciduous, i.e., does not fall away. When the fruit is ripe, it looks like a bag with dried walls (photo G). This fruit opens through two cracks and is called a pod or legume.

The Seed

Study a seed; on its concave side (photo G), a projection, the radicle swelling (1); a long scar, the hilum (2). Between these is a minute opening—the micropyle. If you look at photo F, you will see that the hilum corresponds with the attachment point of the short stalk which joins the seed to the fruit.

If you leave the seed in water overnight to soften it, you will be able to remove a small skin easily. This is the testa or outer seed coat (H, 1): You will see two identical bodies, the cotyledons (seed leaves). Separate them. Still attached to one of the cotyledons (2) is a small embryo plant, consisting of:

● the radicle (3), a small root.

● the hypocotyl (4), a short stem.

● the plumule, two well-developed leaves hiding a tiny bud.

The bean has a two-cotyledon seed, and is called a dicotyledonous plant (dicot).

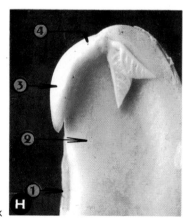

3.5 X

H

8

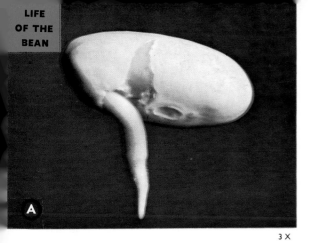

A

3 X

3 X

B

Conclusion

The bean is a herbaceous dicotyledon. Its flower has a bilateral symmetry, a papilionaceous corolla, with free petals. Its fruit is a pod. It belongs to the family *Leguminosae* (from the Latin, *legumen*, pod) and the sub-family of *Papilionaceae*.

LIFE OF THE BEAN

The first stage, the "birth" of the plant, is called germination.

Germination

Place some seeds in damp absorbent cotton-wool, and another lot in a flower pot filled with soil from the garden. To hasten germination, first soak the seeds in water for 24 hours.

Watch the seeds placed in the cotton-wool; you will recognize, among the various phases of development, those that correspond to photos A, B, C and D (above and page 11).

● Photo A. Before reaching this stage, the seed, which is hard and dry and appears to be dead, begins to swell as water enters through the micropyle. A split soon appears in the testa, at the micropyle. The young root grows rapidly. It bears, near its tip, very fine hairs, root hairs, which play an important part in the absorption of water by the plant.

● Photo B. Small swellings appear above the root hairs; these are preliminary shapes of secondary roots. The hypocotyl (1) lengthens.

From this time on, also watch what happens in the flower pot.

● Photo C. The hypocotyl begins to come out of the soil and turns green. The effect of its lengthening is to lift the cotyledons above the ground. The cotyledons begin to separate, and two small green leaves appear. The root system is now well developed.

● Photo D. The hypocotyl straightens and lengthens. The leaves develop and stretch out broadly. These first two leaves are simple and opposed; between their petioles the terminal bud emerges. While these transformations have been taking place, you will have noticed that the cotyledons shrivel away. This is proof that they contained food reserves that were utilized by the young plant. (The food stored, as starches, is changed into soluble glucose by the enzyme diastase for utilization by the young plant until it is able to carry on its own photosynthetic process.)

We have assumed that your beans have germinated normally. For germination to take place, certain conditions must exist. An experiment will demonstrate this.

Take 6 pots, fill them with soil, and number them 1 to 6. At a seed shop, buy some dwarf beans (and if possible, some older beans from at least two years ago). Put the old beans in pot 6 and the younger ones in the other pots. Put the same number of beans in each pot.

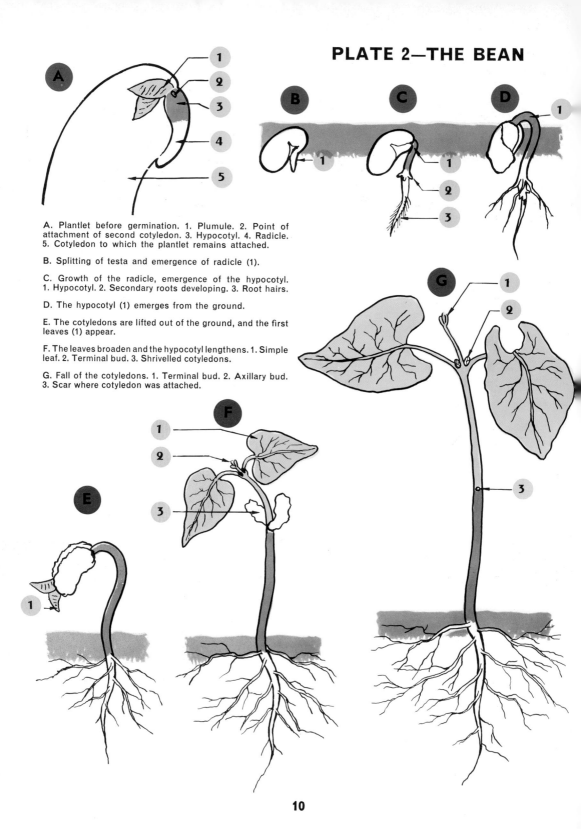

PLATE 2—THE BEAN

A. Plantlet before germination. 1. Plumule. 2. Point of attachment of second cotyledon. 3. Hypocotyl. 4. Radicle. 5. Cotyledon to which the plantlet remains attached.

B. Splitting of testa and emergence of radicle (1).

C. Growth of the radicle, emergence of the hypocotyl. 1. Hypocotyl. 2. Secondary roots developing. 3. Root hairs.

D. The hypocotyl (1) emerges from the ground.

E. The cotyledons are lifted out of the ground, and the first leaves (1) appear.

F. The leaves broaden and the hypocotyl lengthens. 1. Simple leaf. 2. Terminal bud. 3. Shrivelled cotyledons.

G. Fall of the cotyledons. 1. Terminal bud. 2. Axillary bud. 3. Scar where cotyledon was attached.

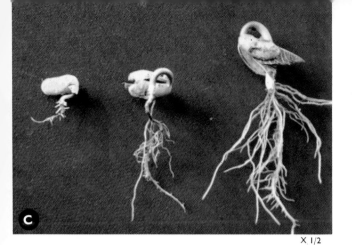

C

X 1/2

D

X 1/2

Tightly pack the soil in pot 2. Bury the beans deeply into pot 3. Place pot 1 on the outside ledge of a window so that it is at a low temperature. Leave all the other pots in a warm room. Water all the pots regularly, except pot 4.

Note, day by day, the number of beans germinating in each pot. Record your observations.

NUMBER OF GERMINATIONS OBSERVED				
Dates				
Pot 1 in the cold				
Pot 2 packed soil				
Pot 3 buried beans				
Pot 4 dry soil				
Pot 5 normal				
Pot 6 old beans				

The results of the experiment should be as follows: The old beans will have lost some of their power of germinating. The others cannot

E

X 1/2

11

F

3 X

After pollination, the flower will fade, although the union of the living substance of the pollen grains with that of the ovules causes fertilization to take place.

Fruition

After fertilization, the wilted flower parts (petals and stamens) fall. Only the calyx and pistil remain, more specifically the ovary, as the major part of the style falls. As shown in the photos on page 6, it is the ovary that changes into the fleshy-walled fruit, then into a dried fruit. You will also see that it is the ovules which change into seeds. When the fruit is ripe (photo G), it opens through two vents, its valves buckle and the seeds it contains fall.

As the flower produces seeds, and a seed is able to produce a new plant, we may assume that the flower constitutes the reproductive system. The calyx and corolla, which play no part in the formation of the fruit and seeds, are simple floral whorls, called the perianth. The stamens are the male organs and the pistils the female organs.

Death of the Plant

About four months after germination, the bean plant which has borne fruit begins to turn yellow, and then all its vegetative system dies. Only its seeds survive in a dormant state, until the moment when, under suitable conditions, they germinate. The bean, which ends its cycle of development in less than a year and dies after fruiting, is an annual plant.

germinate if the soil is packed and lacks air, if they are buried too deeply, or if they lack warmth or moisture.

Growth

The cotyledons have fallen (photo E) leaving a scar on the stem where they were attached (1). But the plant continues to grow: the young plant, whose organs are now well developed, is able to "feed" itself. We can conclude that the roots and the leaves through photosynthetic activity must play an important part in the nutrition of the plant. We know that a plant will die if its roots are cut or its leaves systematically removed.

Compare photo E with photo D. The stem below the cotyledons, the part resulting from the development of the hypocotyl has stopped growing. But, above this point the plant has continued to grow. However, to demonstrate the rôle of the terminal bud, cut it and the plant will stop growing.

In the course of development, the first compound leaves appear. A little later, the axillary buds begin producing secondary stems. Finally, the first flowers will appear.

Flowering

The flowers first appear in the form of small buds which bloom progressively. When the stamens are ripe, the anthers open and the pollen falls on the stigma. This fall of pollen on the stigma, clearly visible in the pea flower in photo F, is called pollination, In this case, as the transport of pollen takes place between organs of the same flower, the pollination is direct (self-pollination).

G

X 1/2

THE TULIP

In late spring, this plant brightens up the flower beds of parks and gardens. Originating in Turkey, the tulip was introduced in the 16th century to Holland, where bulb production is still a substantial source of revenue.

If you uproot a flowering tulip carefully (photo A) you will see:

AN AERIAL PART comprised of a single herbaceous stem, cylindrical, ending in a flower. This stem bears 3 (or 4) simple leaves, complete, without petiole, slightly sheathlike, with parallel veins.

AN UNDERGROUND PART, swollen, with numerous roots running from it: this is the bulb. If you cut this bulb (photo B), you will see that it comprises:

● A brownish base, the stem (1), which extends to the aerial shoot. This short stem bears the roots, which, developing on a stem, are called adventitious roots.

● Interlocked scales. Being borne on the stem, these are leaves, but have a special appearance. At this stage of development, the

X 0.8

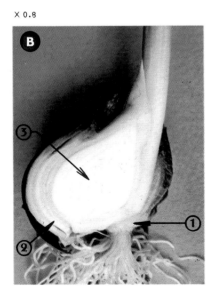

X 1/3

outside scales are brownish, and partly detached from the stem: clearly, they are dead scales (2). The inside scales (3) are white, thick, and fleshy; although carried on the same stem, or plate, these differ from the other scales in having a lighter color. This is a young bulb.

The Flower

The stem bears a single solitary flower. If you study photo A and the close-up of the

13

C

I X

The Fruit and the Seed

After fertilization, the gynoecium remains. The ovary develops and changes into a dry fruit (photo E), which opens through three cracks. Such a fruit is called a capsule. Each cell opens in the middle. The ovules develop into seeds that only have a single cotyledon. Therefore the tulip is a monocotyledon (mono-cot).

LIFE OF THE TULIP

After fertilization, the aerial parts dry up and die. Of the underground part, only a bulb with-out roots remains. The young bulb, shown in photo B, has completed its development. It is covered by dried scales, the remains of the bulb

middle of photo C, you will observe that each flower comprises:

- A whorl of three colored parts (1 in A).
- A second whorl of three similar parts (2 in A) which alternate with the preceding ones. These 6 parts constitute the perianth.
- 6 stamens (photo C), divided into two alternate groups. The anther is comprised of two sacs which contain the pollen.
- A gynoecium whose long ovary bears a short style ending in a voluminous 3-lobed stigma. A cross-section of this ovary (photo D) shows 3 cells (1), each containing two rows of ovules (2). We can conclude that the gynoecium is made up of three fused pistils. The ovary is superior.

Since the parts of the flower can be cut by six radii and a circle (see page 106) the tulip has a radial symmetry.

E

I X

from which it developed. Left in the ground, this bulb will produce a new plant the following spring, and also a new bulb. The tulip is there-fore a plant that can survive the winter because of its bulb.

If you cut this new bulb when it becomes mature (photo F), you will see:

- A stem (1) on which adventitious roots develop in springtime.
- Scales full of food stores. These scales will use up their starch food reserves as the aerial organs develop.
- A large bud, which in the course of de-

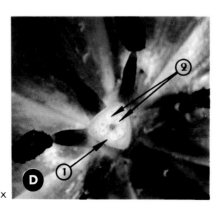

D 1

I X

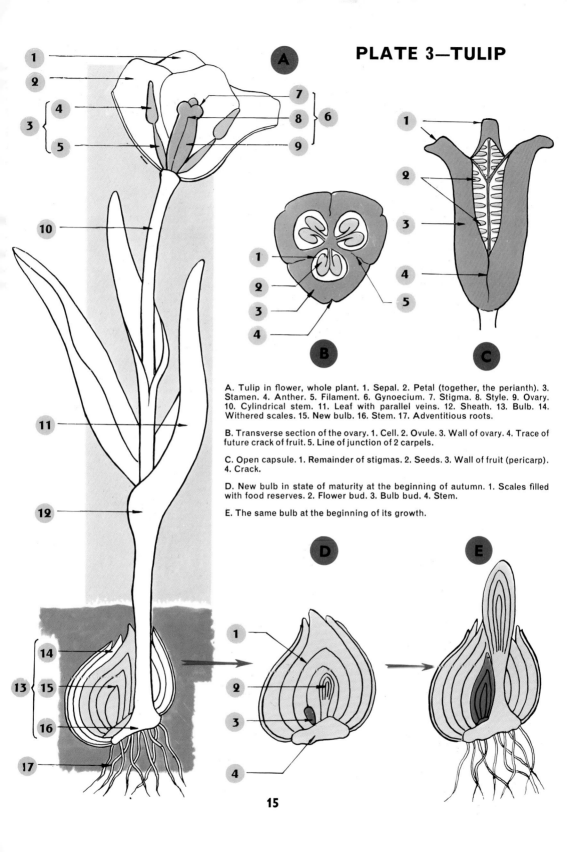

PLATE 3—TULIP

A. Tulip in flower, whole plant. 1. Sepal. 2. Petal (together, the perianth). 3. Stamen. 4. Anther. 5. Filament. 6. Gynoecium. 7. Stigma. 8. Style. 9. Ovary. 10. Cylindrical stem. 11. Leaf with parallel veins. 12. Sheath. 13. Bulb. 14. Withered scales. 15. New bulb. 16. Stem. 17. Adventitious roots.

B. Transverse section of the ovary. 1. Cell. 2. Ovule. 3. Wall of ovary. 4. Trace of future crack of fruit. 5. Line of junction of 2 carpels.

C. Open capsule. 1. Remainder of stigmas. 2. Seeds. 3. Wall of fruit (pericarp). 4. Crack.

D. New bulb in state of maturity at the beginning of autumn. 1. Scales filled with food reserves. 2. Flower bud. 3. Bulb bud. 4. Stem.

E. The same bulb at the beginning of its growth.

15

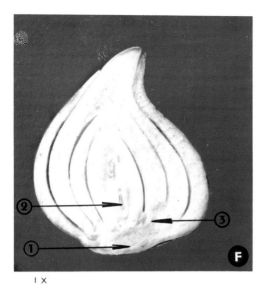

I X

velopment produces a flowering stem: this is the flower bud (2).

● A smaller bud which develops into a new bulb: this is the bulb bud (3).

Conclusion

The tulip is a monocotyledon, perennial because of its bulb. Like most monocotyledons, it has leaves with parallel veins. Its flower is regular. Its fruit is a capsule. The tulip, whose flower is of the same type as that of the Lily, belongs to the family *Liliaceae*.

SOME PLANTS OF THE LILIACEOUS FAMILY

All the plants included in this family, like the tulip, have seeds with a single cotyledon, and a colorful perianth.

Liliaceous plants are divided into:

Liliacea with Capsule and Bulb:

● The lilies, such as the cultivated Martagon lily shown in photo G. This lily grows in a wild state in the Alps, where it flowers in July.
● The hyacinths, whose sepals and petals are fused.

● The garlic, onion, shallot, and leek, which are well known food plants.
● The meadow-saffron (*Colchicum autumnale*), a poisonous plant with fused sepals and petals. This plant flowers in autumn, but its fruit does not appear until mid-spring. This fruit opens through three cracks, situated between the carpels.

Liliacea with Berries and Rhizomes:

● The well known lily-of-the-valley (*Convallaria majalis*), whose sepals and petals are fused.
● Solomon's seal (*Polygonatum biflorum* and *Polygonatum multiflorum*) which flowers in shady places. Its petals and sepals are fused the aerial stem in falling leaves a scar on the rhizome in the shape of a seal (hence, its name).
● The Herb Paris (*Paris quadrifolia*), which has 4 leaves attached at the same point to the stem. Its black berry is poisonous.

X 1/2

THE BUTTERCUP

There are many species of *Ranunculus*. From early spring to early autumn they brighten damp localities with their golden-yellow flowers. One among them, the buttercup or crowfoot, has a bitter taste and poisonous properties.

VEGETATIVE SYSTEM

On the complete plant shown in photo A (*Ranunculus acris*) you can see:

AN UNDERGROUND PART, consisting of a brown, knotty organ, with numerous roots running from it. The buds found on this organ show that it develops from an underground stem. Such a stem is called a rhizome (2). All such roots which grow on a stem are called adventitious roots (1).

AN AERIAL PART, comprised of a green, herbaceous branching stem (4) bearing alternate leaves and flowers. Note that the bottom leaves have a long petiole, a denticulate margin and a large sheath (3) enveloping the stem: these are ensheathed leaves. The upper leaves are more simple. The nearer to the top of the plant, the simpler they become.

NOTE: the *Ranunculaceae* owe their name to their habitat, damp localities, frequented by frogs—the Latin *ranunculus* means little frog.

The Flower

Photo A shows that the main stem and branches all end in a flower.

Try to pull apart the different parts of a flower. Alternatively, look at photo A and the cut flower, photo B. Note that each flower comprises:

● A calyx made up of 5 green, free sepals.

● A corolla made up of 5 petals, golden-yellow and free. At the bottom of each petal, you can see a scale (1 in B) which covers a small cavity, full of the sweet juice or nectar sought after by insects.

● Numerous stamens. Observe that the swollen part of the anthers (2) points towards the exterior.

17

4 X   5 X

● A gynoecium composed of numerous free, superior carpels (4). These are attached to the curved part of the receptacle (3). Each carpel (photo C) comprises an ovary (1) with a single ovule, a very short style (2) and a crooked stigma (3).

All the parts of the flower, sepals, petals, stamens and carpels, are arranged one after the other on the receptacle, thus forming a tight spiral. Thus, the buttercup has a spiral symmetry. Its floral diagram is pictured on page 106.

The Fruit and the Seed

The buttercup is a dicotyledon. After fertilization, the flower wilts, the different parts fall, and only the carpels remain (photo D).

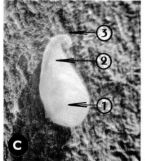

X 1/2

Each carpel becomes a dry fruit that does not open, and such a fruit is called an achene. In the buttercup, which possesses numerous achenes, each contains only one small seed.

When mature, the fruits fall. Because of their hooked ends, they may become attached to the hair of animals and thus carried some way from the plant. This brings about dispersal of the seeds, and therefore of the plant.

LIFE OF THE BUTTERCUP

In winter, the aerial parts die and the rhizome lies dormant until the following spring. At this time, the terminal bud grows and produces a new rhizome on which new aerial shoots appear. During this period, the old parts of the rhizome die. By means of its rhizome, the buttercup reproduces itself in the same place for many years, and is said to be a perennial plant. The seeds that have lain dormant now germinate, bursting the walls of the fruit.

Conclusion

The buttercup is a herbaceous, perennial dicotyledon. It has a flower with spiral symmetry, free petals, numerous stamens and anthers turned towards the exterior. Its fruits are composed of numerous achenes. The buttercup belongs to the family *Ranunculaceae*.

18

PLATE 4—BUTTERCUP

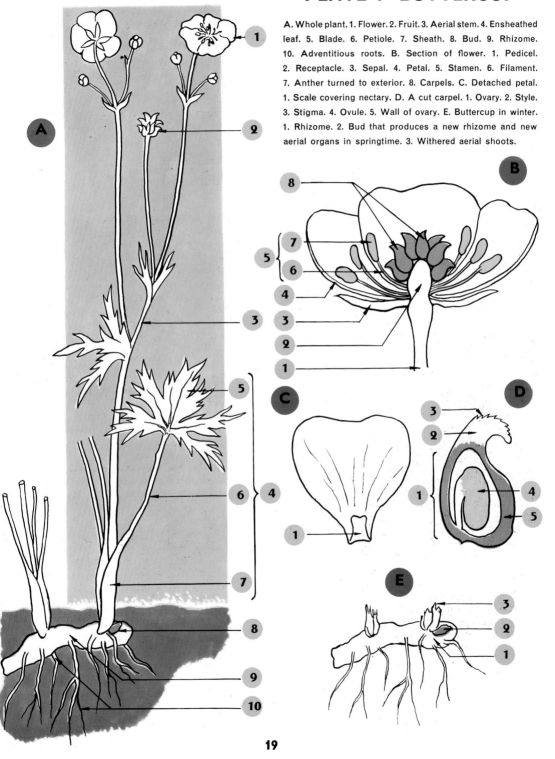

A. Whole plant. 1. Flower. 2. Fruit. 3. Aerial stem. 4. Ensheathed leaf. 5. Blade. 6. Petiole. 7. Sheath. 8. Bud. 9. Rhizome. 10. Adventitious roots. B. Section of flower. 1. Pedicel. 2. Receptacle. 3. Sepal. 4. Petal. 5. Stamen. 6. Filament. 7. Anther turned to exterior. 8. Carpels. C. Detached petal. 1. Scale covering nectary. D. A cut carpel. 1. Ovary. 2. Style. 3. Stigma. 4. Ovule. 5. Wall of ovary. E. Buttercup in winter. 1. Rhizome. 2. Bud that produces a new rhizome and new aerial organs in springtime. 3. Withered aerial shoots.

19

THE MAPLE

The sycamore maple (*Acer pseudo-platanus*) shown in photo A is found growing individually or in small clusters and seldom forms real forests. It is commonly used as a hedge row tree and as a border for streets and highways.

The maple tree grows rapidly. When isolated (photo A), it can reach 100 feet in height. Its crown, a fine oval, has a dense foliage which from a distance has the appearance of a plane tree.

VEGETATIVE SYSTEM

AN UNDERGROUND PART consists of a tap root and numerous secondary roots. The depth of root penetration depends on the thickness of the layer of loose soil.

AN AERIAL PART. The trunk, often short, has a smooth bark in the young tree. If the tree is old, the dead parts of the bark come off in patches. The branches are very numerous; they turn at their ends and spread out broadly.

The leaves (photo B) are simple, opposite, and only borne by young branches. They have a long petiole whose base, or sheath, is wide. Their blade is dark and shiny on its upper surface, lighter and dull on its lower surface. The veins are prominent and 5 principal veins all lead from the same point; thus, the venation is said to be palmate.

X 1/150

X 1/6

An oval lobe corresponds with each principal vein, and has numerous small, rounded serrations. Observe in photo B that the leaves scarcely overlap, permitting them to spread out widely so that each can receive the maximum of light. In autumn, the leaves are often covered with round, black stains produced by a fungal parasite. NOTE: The structure of the vegetative system will be studied along with the cherry (page 24).

The Flowers

Towards the middle of spring, the leaf and flower buds burst, almost simultaneously. The flowers (photo C) grouped into pendant racemes, are small and greenish-yellow. Hidden by the young leaves, they are only recognizable if the branches are closely observed.

Upon careful examination of a cut flower (photo D), note that it has:

- A calyx formed of 4 or 5 green, free sepals.
- A corolla comprising 4 or 5 yellowish free petals, alternating with the sepals.
- An androecium of 8 free stamens. At the base of each is a gland which secretes a highly perfumed nectar, popular with bees. Therefore pollination of the maple is carried out by insects.
- A superior gynoecium, formed of 2 fused carpels, as shown by the presence of 2 stigmas.

The flower of the maple is therefore a complete, regular flower (see page 106).

The Fruit and the Seed

After fertilization, the calyx, corolla, and stamens wither and fall. Only the 2 fused carpels remain, swell up and each gives birth to a dry fruit which does not open (photo E). The fruit of the maple consists of 2 fused parts. In developing, each fruit equips itself with a samara, or dry membrane shaped like a wing (1), which allows it to fly in the wind like a helicopter rotor. With two wings, the fruit of the maple is a di-samara. The wind, moving the raceme of fruits, detaches the di-samaras gradually and carries them away, assuring dispersal of the fruit. The two wings of the sycamore maple's fruit are not widely separated from one another, and distinguish this tree from other maples.

Each fruit (photo E) contains only a single seed (2), covered with a fine down that protects it from the hardships of winter. This seed, cut lengthwise, reveals a two-cotyledon plantlet (3), green, and rolled up on itself. The maple is therefore a dicotyledon.

LIFE OF THE MAPLE

In the autumn, the di-samaras are scattered by the wind, the leaves fall, leaving a leaf scar on the stem, and the tree looks dead. The maple is a tree with deciduous leaves. But if you examine a branch in the autumn you will observe that it bears young, opposite buds in pairs.

X 1/2

These buds are long, pointed, and are equipped with numerous scales with the most external ones having a protective function. In spring, they will open out and will form either a young, leaf-bearing branch, or an inflorescence.

The seed, whose cover is softened by winter snow and rain, swells and bursts the wall of the fruit (photo F). The two cotyledons, freed, remain on the ground, and for some time are oddly capped with the remains of the winged achene. Long and narrow, swollen with food, they bear no resemblance to the adult leaves. The radicle sinks into the soil and the coty-

7 X

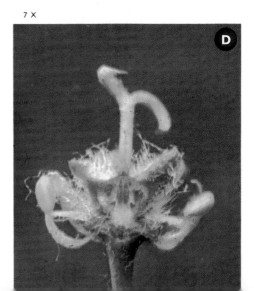

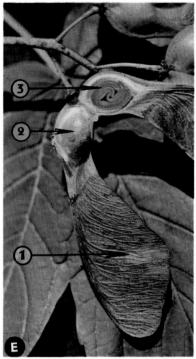

1,5 X

1 X

ledons slowly wither. The plumule forms the second pair of opposed leaves. These already have the typical appearance of the sycamore maple leaf.

Conclusion

The sycamore maple is an arborescent dicotyledon. The deciduous leaves are opposite and have five main veins. The complete flowers are grouped in pendant racemes. The fruit is a winged di-samara.

The sycamore maple belongs to the family *Aceraceae* (from the Latin, *acer*, maple).

SOME PLANTS OF THE FAMILY ACERACEAE

This family comprises only one genus, but a number of species, which like the sycamore maple, all have:

- A two-cotyledon seed.
- Di-samaras grouped in racemes.

Among the plants of this family:

The Norway maple (*Acer platanoides*) is often mingled with the sycamore maple in forests. The serrations of the leaves are few and pointed. The foliage is lighter than that of the sycamore maple, whose leaves strongly resemble those of the Norway maple, but only have three main veins. The di-samaras have wings forming an obtuse angle and the fruits are flattened, while those of the sycamore maple form an acute angle and are rounded.

The hedge maple (*Acer campestre*) is the smallest of the three maples in this section. It is found mainly in undergrowth. Its small, dark leaves have very rounded lobes, devoid of serrations. The wings of the di-samaras form such an open angle that the fruit is perpendicular to its stalk.

The sugar maple (*Acer saccharum*), a fine looking tree with large, attractively denticulated leaves, is very abundant in the forests of Canada and the temperate regions of the United States. It is famous for its sweet sap from which maple syrup and sugar is made.

22

PLATE 5—MAPLE

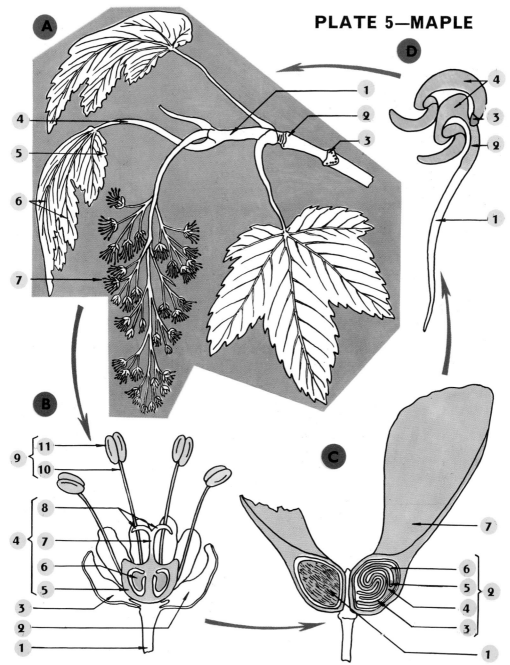

A. Branch of sycamore maple in spring. 1. Newly formed shoot. 2. Shoot from previous year. 3. Leaf scar. 4. Petiole. 5. Lobed and serrated margin. 6. Veins. 7. Inflorescence in a raceme. The sycamore maple is recognizable by its leaves, which have 5 principal veins; its lobes have rounded serrations.

B. Section of flower. 1. Pedicel. 2. Sepal. 3. Petal. 4. Gynoecium. 5. Ovary. 6. Ovule. 7. Style. 8. Stigma. 9. Stamen. 10. Filament. 11. Anther.

C. Winged fruit or di-samara, partly cut. 1. Seed covered by down. 2. Seed cut to show embryo. 3. Radicle. 4. Hypocotyl. 5. Plumule. 6. Cotyledons. 7. Wing.

D. Embryo at moment of germination. 1. Radicle. 2. Hypocotyl. 3. Plumule. 4. Cotyledons.

A

I X

THE CHERRY

It is in early spring, when photo A was taken, that the cherry (*Prunus cerasus*) adorns itself first with flowers and then with leaves. Scarcely two months later, small green cherries follow after the flowers, and these later turn into delicious fruits.

VEGETATIVE SYSTEM

Because of its height, robustness and longevity, the cherry, like the sycamore maple, deserves the name of tree or more precisely, that of fruit tree, as it produces edible fruits. Its vegetative system comprises:

AN UNDERGROUND PART, formed of strong roots consisting of a tap root and numerous secondary roots.

AN AERIAL PART, comprised of an upright stem, thick and hard, called a trunk, which divides into numerous branches. The branches bear simple, serrated leaves whose sheath is flanked by two stipules.

The structure can best be seen on a sawed-off branch (photo B), where there is, from the periphery towards the middle, the following:

● A brown layer whose external part separates in ribbons, called the bark (1).

● A lighter layer, not as thick, having a laminated appearance: the phloem (2).

● A thick region, fibrous and firm, with alternately light and dark rings: the xylem, composed of woody tissue. The dark part in the middle is the pith.

On a young branch, like that shown in photo B, the wood comprises a central hard, dry zone, the heart wood (4), and a softer, damper peripheral zone, the sap wood or alburnum (3). The sap wood is moist, as it conducts the sap and represents the living part of the wood.

The Flower

You can see, from photo A, that the flowers are bunched, usually in threes, and all their pedicels run from one point situated in the middle of a rosette of scales. Such an inflorescence is called an umbel.

Dissect a flower, or, if this is not possible, study the cut flower shown in photo C. You can observe that each flower comprises:

- A calyx made up of 5 sepals, green and curved towards the bottom.
- A corolla formed of 5 petals, free, and alternating with the sepals.
- Numerous stamens, differing from the buttercup in that their anthers point towards the interior.
- A gynoecium formed from a single carpel, containing a clearly visible ovary, style and stigma. It is situated in the middle of a cup, to the border of which the other flower parts are attached. This cup is a floral hypanthium.

The flower is regular and has a radial symmetry (see page 106).

The Fruit and the Seed

After fertilization (photo D), the petals fall, but the sepals and stamens remain attached to the receptacle at their base. You will have noticed when dissecting the flower that it is impossible to pull these parts out. The ovary grows and the style wilts. Then (photo E) the ovary bursts from the receptacle, which falls, and a small green cherry appears. The flower of the cherry tree therefore has a deciduous receptacle.

If you slice this small cherry (photo F) you will see, inside, a white, oval-shaped organ; this is the future seed. Around it is the wall of the ovary. Observation of this wall reveals the existence of three layers. In comparing with the fruit (photo G) you can easily see what these three layers are: the very thin skin (epicarp); the flesh, or pulp, full of sweetened juice (mesocarp); the thick, hard-walled pit or stone (endocarp) which surrounds the seed. It is

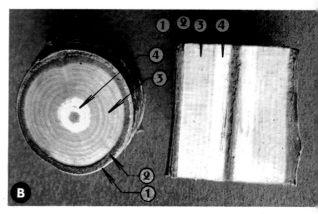

I X

obvious that the "tail" of the cherry is none other than the pedicel which has become lengthened.

The cherry is a fleshy stone fruit. Such a fruit is called a drupe. Because the seed has two cotyledons (1), as can be seen in photo G, the cherry is a dicotyledon.

LIFE OF THE CHERRY TREE

In autumn, the cherry loses its leaves; it is a tree with deciduous leaves. The sap ceases to circulate and the plant appears to be dead. If at this time you examine a branch (photo H), you

3 X

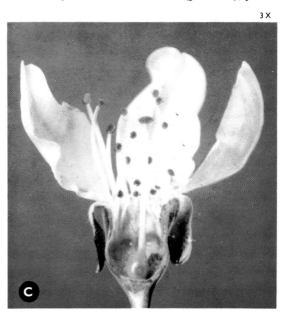

25

2 ×　　　　　　　　2 ×　　　　　　　　2 ×

will see that it bears buds composed on the outside of thick, brown scales covered with a resinous substance; these scales obviously have a protective rôle. The buds are of two types:

- Some, small and pointed, are called spurs, wood or stem buds (1).
- The others, larger and rounder, are flower buds (2).

The spurs are isolated on the branches and the buds grouped.

In springtime, the scales of the buds open up, and the fragile organs that they protected during the cold winter appear. The spurs produce leaves, new branches, and new stem buds. The flower buds produce flowers.

As the new branches appear, the roots, the trunk, and the old branches increase in diameter through the formation of new layers of wood. This explains the presence of the annual rings seen in photo B. Knowing moreover that each new layer of wood has a light part (the wood of spring) and a dark part (the wood of autumn), you can see that it is possible to calculate the age of a tree by counting the annual rings of its trunk.

Conclusion

The cherry tree is a woody, arborescent dicotyledon with deciduous leaves. It has a regular flower with free petals, numerous stamens and anthers turned towards the interior. Its fruit is a drupe. The cherry tree belongs to the family *Rosaceae*.

2 ×

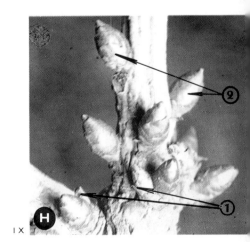

I ×

26

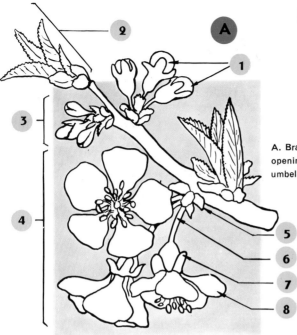

PLATE 6—THE CHERRY TREE

A. Branch in flower. 1. Flowers in bud. 2. Wood bud, or spur, opening out. 3. Flower bud blossoms. 4. Flowers grouped in an umbel. 5. Scales. 6. Pedicel. 7. Sepal. 8. Petal.

B. Section of flower. 1. Pedicel. 2. Hypanthium. 3. Reversed sepal. 4. Petal. 5. Stamen. 6. Filament. 7. Anther turned to interior. 8. Gynoecium. 9. Stigma. 10. Style. 11. Ovary. 12. Ovule.

C. Section of ripe fruit. 1. Pedicel. 2. Skin (epicarp). 3. Flesh or pulp (mesocarp). 4. Stone (endocarp). 5. Two-cotyledon seed. 6. Testa of seed.

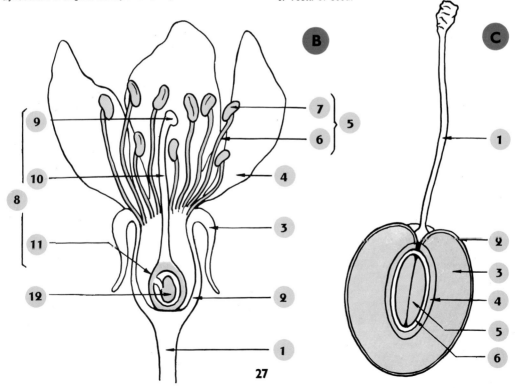

27

X 1/6

B

3 X

C

1 X

THE FAMILY ROSACEAE

All plants in this family, like the cherry, have a two-cotyledon seed, a flower with 5 sepals, 5 free petals, and numerous stamens, with anthers turned to the interior.

Rosaceae with Numerous Carpels Fixed to a Curved Receptacle

One type is the strawberry (*Fragaria vesca*) (photo A): This is a herbaceous plant with the ability to propagate by long creeping stems called runners (1). The cut flower (photo B) shows that the gynoecium is composed of numerous free carpels. In comparing with photo C, you will note that the part we eat is not literally a fruit but the receptacle, which has become fleshy and red and on which are numerous small dry fruits or achenes.

The raspberry (*Rubus idaeus*) belongs to this type, but its receptacle does not become fleshy; instead each of its many carpels becomes a small drupe.

Rosaceae with 5 Carpels Fused to a Hypanthium

The apple tree (*Pyrus malus*) is typical. This is a woody, arborescent plant. In photo D,

you can clearly see the 5 styles with 5 carpels fused to the receptacle, each containing two ovules. Cut an apple in half vertically and you will note the remains of the flower parts; the skin; the flesh (which we eat) that has resulted at one and the same time from the receptacle and the ovary; the parchment walls which are the equivalent of the stone of the cherry; and the pips or seeds originating in the ovules.

Rosaceae with Numerous Carpels Attached to the Bottom of a Hypanthium

These are typified by the wild or dog rose (*Rosa canina*) (photo E), a small, woody plant which flowers in early summer. Its branches are equipped with hooked thorns, or spines. Its leaves are compound pinnate; their petiole is flanked by two long stipules. The cross-section (photo E) shows that each carpel is surmounted by a long style. In comparing the wild rose with the strawberry, note that the red part (photo F), called the fruit, is really a receptacle which has become fleshy, and contains numerous hairy achenes, the true fruits.

1 X

1.5 X

D

E

1 X

F

THE POTATO

The common potato (*Solanum tuberosum*) is a plant which originated in South America and was introduced into Europe in about 1550. At first little appreciated, because its tubers were small and bitter, it was popularized by Parmentier in the 18th century and became widely cultivated. Today, it plays a leading part in our diet.

VEGETATIVE SYSTEM

If you examine a potato plant that has been carefully uprooted (photo A), you will see:

AN AERIAL PART comprised of green, herbaceous stems, which bear alternate compound pinnate leaves. All these organs are poisonous.

AN UNDERGROUND PART, where, in the extension of the aerial stems, you can distinguish brownish organs bearing scaly leaves: these are the underground stems. From these stems run numerous fine, very spread-out roots: these are fibrous adventitious roots. Horizontal, whitish stalks also run from these stems. More or less spreading and equipped with small, scaly leaves, these are rhizomes. Their swollen end, the potato, is a tuber.

If you examine the tuber shown in photo E, you will see small depressions on its surface: the "eyes." Each eye comprises a small scale and three small buds. The tuber is therefore also a stem, but it is a stem swollen with food reserves. It is full of starch grains which are extracted in the form of a powder called *fecula*.

The Flower

Photo B shows an inflorescence and photo C a sectioned flower. Note that each flower comprises:

● A calyx formed of 5 green sepals, fused at their base.

X 1/2

● A corolla formed of 5 completely fused petals alternating with the sepals.

● 5 stamens alternating with the petals and fused at the corolla by their filaments. Their anthers, pressed tightly against one another, form a tube that crosses the style.

● A superior gynoecium, formed of two fused carpels in a two-celled ovary containing numerous ovules. The ovary is surmounted by a style with a swollen stigma.

The regular flower has a radial symmetry (see page 106).

B

X 2/3

C

2 X

The Fruit and the Seed

After fertilization, the ovary changes into a fleshy fruit, first green, then purplish. On the section of this fruit (photo D), you can recognize: the skin (1), the flesh or pulp (2), the seeds or pips (3). This fruit, which has no stone, is a berry. As its seeds have two cotyledons, the potato is a dicotyledon.

LIFE AND CULTIVATION OF THE POTATO

If a tuber is left behind in the ground at potato-lifting time, the following year there will be a new plant, bearing new tubers, in its place. The potato is a plant which is perennial through its tubers. Cultivation of the potato is based on this property. In spring, after turning and fertilizing the soil, we plant tubers already bearing sprouts, as shown in photo E. Each sprout, resulting from a developing bud, consists of a short stem from whose base the adventitious roots develop.

As each stem develops, the tuber shrivels up (photo A, 1). The adventitious roots become more abundant. Horizontal stems appear and, on them, the new tubers. In cultivation,

development of these branches which bear tubers is encouraged by piling soil around the potato plant: this operation is called earthing-up. Lifting and harvesting the tubers takes place in autumn, as soon as the leaves begin to turn yellow.

If the seeds have become ripe, which seldom happens in temperate climates, they can develop into other plants. These plants will only produce small tubers. Therefore, we do not sow the true potato seeds.

Conclusion

The potato is a herbaceous dicotyledon, perennial through its tubers. Its regular flower is characterized by a corolla formed of fused petals. Its fruit is a berry.

The potato belongs to the family *Solanaceae*, from the Latin *solanum*, the name used by Pliny the Elder to designate a kind of edible fungus.

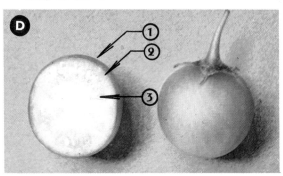

D

(1)
(2)
(3)

X 2/3

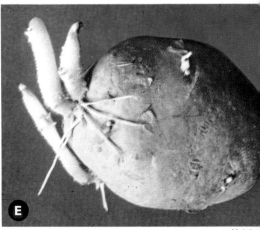

E

X 1/2

30

PLATE 7—THE POTATO

A. Whole plant in flower. 1. Fibrous roots. 2. Old withered tuber. 3. New tuber. 4. Underground rhizome. 5. Underground stem. 6. Scale. 7. Aerial stem. 8. Alternate compound leaves. 9. Flower.

B. 1. Peduncle. 2. Calyx. 3. Corolla. 4. Stamen. 5. Stigma. 6. Style. 7. Ovary. 8. Ovule. 9. Gynoecium.

C. Whole fruit (berry) and sectioned fruit. 1. Calyx. 2. Skin. 3. Pulp. 4. Seed.

D. Germinating tuber. 1. Adventitious roots. 2. Young shoot. 3. Scale leaf. 4. Bud. 5. Scale leaf. 6. Eye.

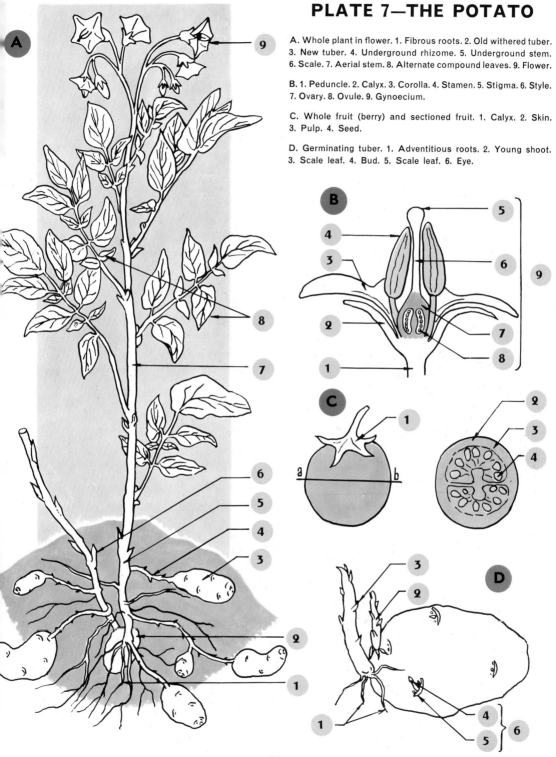

31

THE OAK

X 1/100

VEGETATIVE SYSTEM

Photo A shows that the oak (*Quercus*, sp.) is a large tree (it can reach 130 feet in height and 20 feet in circumference), and has abundant foliage. Its vegetative system comprises:

AN UNDERGROUND PART, by which the tree is so firmly fixed in the ground that it is rarely uprooted. This is, in effect, formed of a long and robust tap root, which divides into numerous secondary roots.

AN AERIAL PART, comprised of a strong trunk, whose upper part bears large, twisting branches, divided into numerous small boughs. The oak in a forest grows in a special way. It spreads less and appears to have a longer trunk, as it loses the branches at its base.

The trunk and branches resemble the branch of a cherry tree. However, the bark of the oak is very thick, gnarled and, cracked.

The leaves, borne by the young branches, are simple, alternate and lobed. In the common oak, with its long peduncles bearing fruits (photo B), the leaves have a very short petiole. In the forest or sessile oak (cl. *Sessiliflora*), whose fruits are not pedunculated (photo G), the leaves are clearly petiolated.

X 2/3

The Flowers

In early spring, oaks that have passed the age of 40 blossom. At this time they bear small flowers grouped in characteristic inflorescences, at the ends of the small branches, and these are of two kinds:

● The first kind has small yellow flowers (photo C) attached in large number to long, hanging peduncles (these are catkins), as well as a calyx (photo D) formed of from 5 to 8 striped sepals, and a variable number (5 to 10) of stamens.

Devoid of a corolla, these are flowers without petals (apetalous flowers). They also lack a gynoecium, so they are male flowers.

● The second kind of inflorescence (photo E) consists of an upright peduncle, ending in 2 or 3 small, greenish flowers. If you cut one of these flowers open, it is clearly fatter, already fruitful, and you will see that it comprises:

● An assembly of small scales, forming a cup, the cupule (1).

32

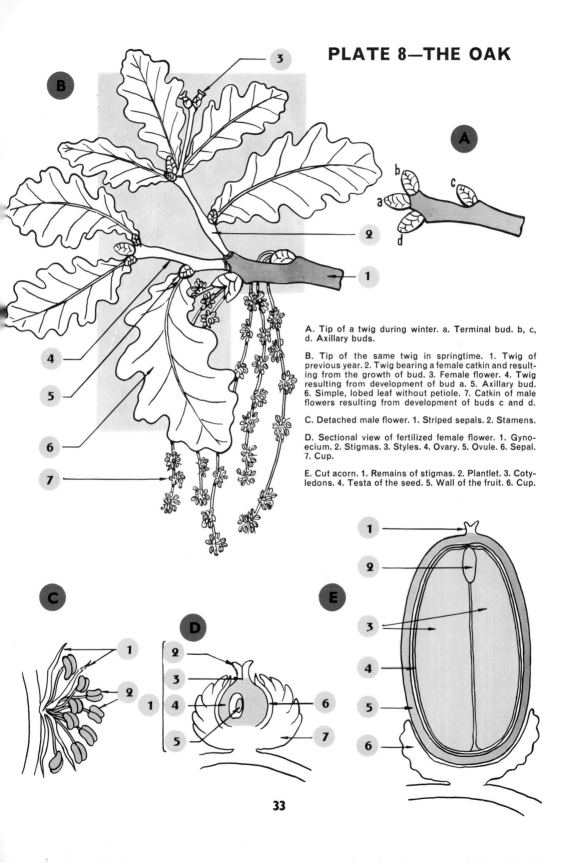

PLATE 8—THE OAK

A. Tip of a twig during winter. a. Terminal bud. b, c, d. Axillary buds.

B. Tip of the same twig in springtime. 1. Twig of previous year. 2. Twig bearing a female catkin and resulting from the growth of bud. 3. Female flower. 4. Twig resulting from development of bud a. 5. Axillary bud. 6. Simple, lobed leaf without petiole. 7. Catkin of male flowers resulting from development of buds c and d.

C. Detached male flower. 1. Striped sepals. 2. Stamens.

D. Sectional view of fertilized female flower. 1. Gynoecium. 2. Stigmas. 3. Styles. 4. Ovary. 5. Ovule. 6. Sepal. 7. Cup.

E. Cut acorn. 1. Remains of stigmas. 2. Plantlet. 3. Cotyledons. 4. Testa of the seed. 5. Wall of the fruit. 6. Cup.

C X 1/2

D

6 X

E

6 X

- A calyx, formed of 6 sepals (2).
- A gynoecium formed of three fused carpels resulting in a globulous ovary (3). Photo E shows that the 3 stigmas are separate; so also are the styles.

These flowers, devoid of corolla, are also apetalous flowers. They also lack stamens, so they are female flowers.

The oak therefore has flowers devoid of petals and lacking either stamens or gynoecium. Such flowers are incomplete flowers.

The Fruit and the Seed

By studying photos E, F, G, H, successively, you will see that after fertilization the ovary changes into an acorn. This acorn grows more quickly than the cup, to which it remains attached until it becomes ripe. The acorn is therefore a single seeded dry fruit, a nut.

Open this nut (photo H). The single seed which has resulted from the development of one of the 6 ovules in the ovary is a large seed with a thin testa (1). Its two cotyledons (2) are fat with food reserves. The oak is therefore a dicotyledon. In photo I, you can see a young plant which has remained attached to one of the cotyledons.

LIFE OF THE OAK

In the autumn, the acorns fall and the oak loses its leaves: it is a tree with deciduous leaves. Its branches, like those of the cherry tree, only bear buds that are encased in protective scales. In spring, these buds produce either male catkins, or leafy twigs, some of which bear female catkins.

Germination of acorns that have fallen to the ground is easy to follow. First of all, the seed swells, causing the wall of the fruit to

6 X

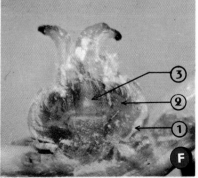

F

G

I X

1.5 X   1.5 X   1 X

burst. Then the root emerges and strikes into the soil (photo J). At the same time, the embryo develops a small stalk (J, 1), but, unlike the bean, the hypocotyl does not lengthen and the cotyledons are not lifted above the ground.

Conclusion

The oak is an arborescent dicotyledon, with deciduous leaves. It has two types of petal-free flowers, one kind male, and the other kind female. Its fruit is a nut, set in a cup. The common oak belongs to the family *Fagaceae*.

SOME PLANTS
OF THE FAMILY FAGACEAE

All the plants of this family have, like the oak:

- A two-cotyledon seed.
- Two kinds of petal-free flowers: One, male (in catkins), the other, female.
- Fruits that are nuts, encased in a cup.

Apart from the oaks, this family comprises:

- The sweet chestnut (*Castanea*, sp.). This tree (photo K) grows on siliceous soils. Its leaves are long, spear-shaped and dentate. The male flowers are grouped in catkins still visible in the photo. The female flowers are grouped at the base of these catkins. The fruits, or chestnuts, are enclosed in cups called burrs, which bristle with long, sharp-pointed spikes. At maturity, each burr opens up through four cracks, releasing the three nuts contained in it.

The chestnut must not be confused with the horse-chestnut tree (*Aesculus hippocastanum*). The horse-chestnut "conker" is a seed, and its burr is a fruit.

- The American beech (*Fagus grandifolia*) (photo L) like its European cousin (*Fagus sylvatica*) is a large tree with a smooth, greyish trunk. Its fruits, or beech nuts, are enclosed in pairs inside a cup, bristling with soft spikes, which splits open through four cracks. Beech nuts are rich in oil.

X 1/4   X 1/2

35

THE CARROT

The cultivated carrot (*Daucus carota*) differs only slightly from the wild carrot ("Queen Anne's Lace") from which it was derived. It is a food plant whose root and leaves are familiar. Its leaves, generally called "tops," give off a characteristic aroma when bruised. But are you familiar with its flowers? Probably not. A study of this plant's cultivation will enable you to understand the reason.

VEGETATIVE SYSTEM

A Young Carrot

Carefully uproot a carrot from the current year's sowing (photo A). You will see:

AN UNDERGROUND PART, comprised of a principal, conical, reddish-orange root, which forces itself into the ground in pivot fashion. This is a tap root and has numerous rootlets running from it. The principal root is large and is filled with stored food; it is a tuberous root.

Cut one of these roots lengthwise (photo A). You will see that it comprises:

● A central, yellow-orange part. This is the wood (1), which, if the carrot has remained too long in the earth, becomes a greenish-yellow, fibrous and hard.

● An orange-red, tender, peripheral zone, with a sweet taste. This is the cortex (2), where the food reserves are accumulated. The cortex is crossed by the rootlets which run from the wood.

● A very thin skin which covers the cortex: the piliferous layer.

AN AERIAL PART comprised of a cluster of deeply divided leaves, which appear to run from the root.

If you look at the longitudinal section of the root, you can see that the leaves are, in fact, borne by a short stem (3) which bears a terminal bud (4).

X 2/3

A Flowering Carrot

If you now study the vegetative system of a flowering carrot (photo B), you will see that:

THE UNDERGROUND PART contains a strong tap root whose wood, more developed, is fibrous and hard, and whose cortex is smaller and shrivelled. It is not sweet and edible.

THE AERIAL PART comprises a long, branched stem, with a ribbed surface, having alternate, sheathed leaves.

The Flower

The flowers are grouped at the end of the branches, in inflorescences of distinctive appearance.

Photo B shows that an inflorescence comprises several large peduncles (1) running from a crown of denticulated bracts called involucre (2). It is an umbel, like the cherry; but at the end of each large peduncle there is a rosette of small bracts (3) forming an involucel, from which run small peduncles, each ending in a flower. Each large peduncle therefore ends in a small secondary umbel or umbellule (4).

The inflorescence of the carrot is an umbel composed of umbellules, or, more simply, a compound umbel.

The length of the peduncles is such that the flowers are to a considerable extent in the same plane.

The flowers are very small, but clearly visible on the part of the umbellule shown magnified in photo C. At the stage of development at which this photo was taken you cannot see all the parts of the flower which comprise:

- A calyx of 5 sepals reduced at the tips.
- A corolla formed of 5 white, free petals.
- 5 stamens, already fallen, but easy to see on a younger flower. The stamens develop before the pistil, which makes cross-fertilization necessary.

The stamens, like the sepals and petals, are fixed to the edge of a hollow receptacle covered with hairs.

- A pistil formed of two carpels, each containing an ovule. The ovary is fused to the receptacle, but the styles and stigmas remain free. They emerge from a curved disc which produces nectar.

The Fruit and the Seed

After flowering, the peduncles of the inflorescences contract, as you can see in the magnified umbellule shown in photo D. Each flower has become a dry fruit whose external wall, bristling with spikes, is in fact the wall of the receptacle. When mature (photo E) the fruit divides into two halves which do not open. The fruit of the carrot is formed of two mericarps: it is a cremocarp.

Because each mericarp contains a two-cotyledon seed, the carrot is a dicotyledon.

10 X

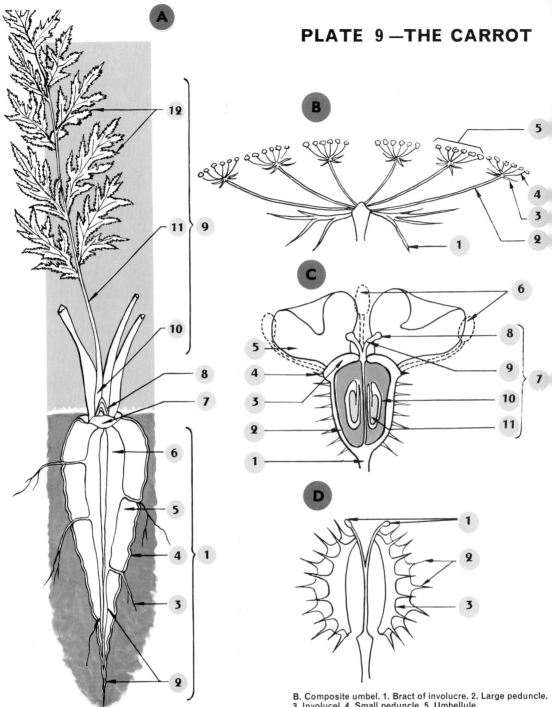

PLATE 9 — THE CARROT

A. Root cut lengthwise. 1. Tap root. 2. Principal root. 3. Rootlets. 4. Piliferous layer. 5. Cortex. 6. Wood. 7. Stem. 8. Terminal bud. 9. Sheathed leaf. 10. Sheath. 11. Petiole. 12. Denticulate leaves.

B. Composite umbel. 1. Bract of involucre. 2. Large peduncle. 3. Involucel. 4. Small peduncle. 5. Umbellule.
C. Section of flower (after fall of stamens). 1. Floral peduncle. 2. Hollow receptacle fused to the ovary. 3. Nectar disc. 4. Sepal. 5. Petal. 6. Position of stamens. 7. Pistil. 8. Stigma. 9. Style. 10. Ovary. 11. Ovule.
D. Ripe fruit. 1. Remaining styles. 2. Stiff points (wall of receptacle). 3. Mericarp.

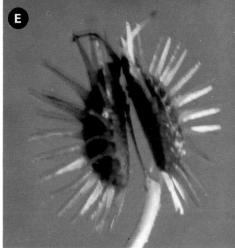

5 X   10 X

CULTIVATION AND LIFE OF THE CARROT

The cultivation of this plant, which is very widespread, involves some of the same operations that are used for the bean.

Harvesting

The plant, provided with an abundant foliage, known as tops, accumulates food reserves in its root which thus becomes a swollen tap root. Carrots intended for consumption are lifted at this stage. Their aerial part (photo A) only consists of leaves and a small stem.

Fruiting

Suppose we leave some carrots in the ground. In autumn the leaves die, but the root and stem survive. The following spring, the small stem and its terminal bud develop; an aerial stem, leaves, then flowers appear (photo F). As these aerial organs develop, the root uses up its food reserves. Then, after having fruited, the whole plant dies.

The full development of the cultivated carrot is therefore stretched over two years: it is a biennial plant. The first year, it develops like a plant that is perennial through its root.

In cultivation, the market gardeners who produce their own carrot seed never leave the roots in the earth during winter, for fear of frost. They pull them up and replant them in the spring.

Conclusion

The carrot is a herbaceous, biennial dicotyledon, with a tuberous tap root. Its free-petalled flowers are grouped in compound umbels. Its fruits are formed of two mericarps. The carrot belongs to the family *Umbelliferae*.

X 1/20

THE DANDELION

The dandelion (*Taraxacum officinale*) is a common plant which flowers from spring to autumn. It is well known through its leaves, which are sometimes eaten in salads, and by the feathery balls of its fruits which separate at the slightest breath of wind.

VEGETATIVE SYSTEM

Photo A shows a complete plant from which one leaf has been removed to make the flower buds more visible. You can see:

AN UNDERGROUND PART, comprised of a principal tap root, and rootlets. If this root is broken, a milky liquid of bitter taste oozes out.

AN AERIAL PART, comprised of a very short stem whose leaves form a rosette close to the ground. The leaves have a blade cut into sharp-pointed teeth, from which comes the name—Dent-de-lion, meaning "lion teeth."

The Flower

You can see, in the middle of the rosette of leaves, a flower bud. This bud will later be borne on a long hollow stalk, or floral scape.

When the bud opens (photo B), a large number of small yellow flowers appear. They are all alike. The "flower" of the dandelion is therefore not a flower, but an inflorescence; it is a composite flower. The green parts surrounding these flowers are not sepals, but involucres (1).

X 1/3

On a cut inflorescence (photo C) you can verify that the flowers are attached to the broadened, slightly curved end of the floral scape. Such an inflorescence is a capitulum, or small head. Note that the flowers in the middle are still in bud.

Pull an opened-out flower from the outer surface (photo D); you will see that it is comprised of:

● A crown of fine hairs (pappus), many in number, comparable to a calyx.

● A whitish tube, which extends, on one side, to a ligule with 5 teeth. This is an irregular corolla, which gives the flower a bilateral symmetry. It is formed of 5 fused petals. The characteristic appearance of the corolla has resulted in this flower receiving the name of tongued flower.

2 X

40

C   2 X

D   6 X

● Five stamens born by the corolla, alternate with the petals. The fused anthers (D, 1), form a tube which crosses the style (2).

● A gynoecium comprising an ovary (3), a long style and a stigma with two coiled lobes. These two lobes show that the gynoecium is formed of two fused carpels. However, the ovary only has a single ovule, situated below the point of attachment of the other flower parts: it is an inferior ovary.

The Fruit and the Seed

After blossoming, the flowers wilt and the bracts contract, as you can see in photo A, 1. A little later, the bracts burst open again, and you see the silky ball of fruits open out; in photo E, some of the fruits have been blown off by the wind. This photo shows that each flower has become a light fruit comprising:

● A swollen part, the fruit proper, which is a cypsela.

● A stem ending in a tuft of hairs forming a parachute. These hairs, which come out of the calyx, help to carry the seeds considerable distances. Because the seed has two cotyledons, the dandelion is a dicotyledon.

LIFE OF THE DANDELION

In winter, the aerial parts of the plant die, but the root continues to live and it produces a new plant in spring. The dandelion is a plant which is perennial through its roots.

Conclusion

The dandelion is a herbaceous, perennial dicotyledon. Its flowers, grouped in capitulums, are all tongue-shaped flowers, with fused petals and with stamens fused by their anthers. Its fruits are cypselas. The dandelion belongs to the family *Compositae* (plants whose "flowers" are composite flowers).

I X

E

41

X 1/4

SOME PLANTS OF THE FAMILY COMPOSITAE

All the plants included in this family, like the dandelion, have stamens fused by their anthers; a gynoecium formed of two carpels fused in an inferior ovary; and fruits which are cypselas. Most of the plants of this family belong to one of the three following groups:

Composite Flowers with Strap-Shaped Corolla

Like the dandelion, all these plants have inflorescences formed solely of flowers:

The lettuce (*Lactuca sativa*) and the endive (*Cichorium endivia*), whose leaves are eaten.

The salsify (*Tragopogon porrifolius*), whose root is eaten.

The wild chicory (*Cichorium intybus*), one variety of which is cultivated for its root (photo A). This plant has a stiff, branched stem and is common along roadsides. It can be recognized by its blue (sometimes white) flowers which appear from early summer to mid-autumn.

Composites with Tube-Shaped Flowers

The cornflower, Bachelor's Button or Blue Bottle (*Centaurea cyanus*) is a plant common along roadsides and in cornfields, flowering in summer (photo B). Its inflorescences are formed of two kinds of flowers, shown detached in photo C:

● The inner flowers (1) have a tube-shaped corolla, with 5 lobes, formed of 5 fused petals.

● The outer flowers (2), are larger and have a tube-shaped corolla which widens out at the mouth into a kind of trumpet with 7 teeth.

These flowers without either stamens or gynoecium are sterile flowers. Like the cornflower,

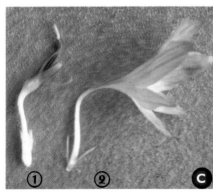

X 1/2

① ②

C

I X

X 1/5

D

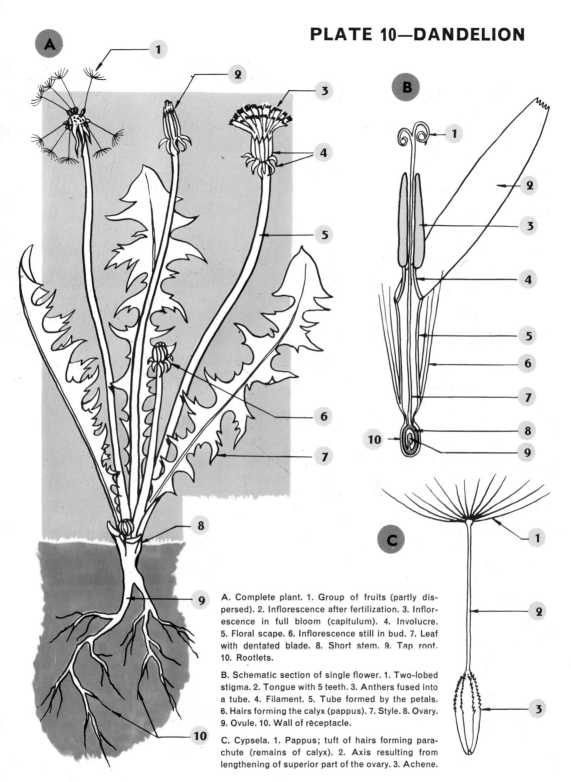

PLATE 10—DANDELION

A. Complete plant. 1. Group of fruits (partly dispersed). 2. Inflorescence after fertilization. 3. Inflorescence in full bloom (capitulum). 4. Involucre. 5. Floral scape. 6. Inflorescence still in bud. 7. Leaf with dentated blade. 8. Short stem. 9. Tap root. 10. Rootlets.

B. Schematic section of single flower. 1. Two-lobed stigma. 2. Tongue with 5 teeth. 3. Anthers fused into a tube. 4. Filament. 5. Tube formed by the petals. 6. Hairs forming the calyx (pappus). 7. Style. 8. Ovary. 9. Ovule. 10. Wall of receptacle.

C. Cypsela. 1. Pappus; tuft of hairs forming parachute (remains of calyx). 2. Axis resulting from lengthening of superior part of the ovary. 3. Achene.

43

E

all in this group have inflorescences formed solely of tube-shaped flowers, such as:

The burdock (*Arctium lappa*), which grows on waste ground and flowers (photo D) from early summer to mid-autumn. Its capitulums attach themselves easily to clothes because of small hooks located at the ends of the bracts.

The thistles, such as the carline thistle (*Carlina vulgaris*) shown in photo E.

All are characterized by the presence of prickly leaves.

Composites with Two Kinds of Flowers

The ox-eye or white daisy (*Chrysanthemum leucanthemum*) has capitulums (photo F) which bear two kinds of flowers. These have been detached and greatly magnified in photo G.

● The middle flowers are small and yellow, similar to the middle flowers of the cornflower. These are tube-shaped, but their calyx is reduced.

● The outer flowers are strap-shaped, white, and similar to those of the dandelion. But their calyx is reduced, their ligule has only three teeth and they have no stamens.

Like the ox-eye daisy, the plants of this group have inflorescences consisting at one and the same time of tube-shaped flowers and strap-shaped flowers. Such plants are:

The arnica (*Arnica montana*) whose strap-shaped flowers are yellow (photo H). This is a mountain plant which flowers in mid-summer.

F

2 ×

G

10 ×

H

× 1/5

44

WHEAT

Grains of wheat found on prehistoric sites prove that this plant has been known to man since earliest times. In the present day, this cereal plays an important part in the diet of man and animals.

VEGETATIVE SYSTEM

Study a wheat plant (*Triticum aestivum* or *Triticum vulgare*) which has been carefully uprooted (photo A). You will see that it comprises:

AN AERIAL PART composed of several long herbaceous stems, cylindrical, slender, unbranched, swollen at the nodes. On a longitudinal section, you will see that these stems are solid at the nodes, and hollow in the internodes. Called culms, they are supple and strong.

You will note from photos A and C that the leaves are alternate and that a leaf comprises:

● A long sheath, covering for most of its length the internode above its point of attachment. The leaves are therefore ensheathed.

● A blade with parallel veins, long and straight. At its junction with the sheath, note (photo C) a small tongue called the ligula (1).

AN UNDERGROUND PART, comprising (photo B) branched stems, with very short internodes whose nodes (1) bear numerous adventitious

× 1/5

A

roots. The fibrous root system of the wheat plant is formed of roots that are all equally developed and spread out.

The Flower

The flowers are grouped at the end of the stems in inflorescences called ears (photo C). If you look at an ear head-on (a) and in profile (b) you will see that it is made up of several similar parts (3). The axis of the ear, bared (2) presents a zig-zag appearance because of the alternation of the small stalks (removed).

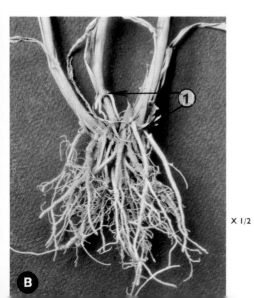

× 1/2

B

45

× 1/2

6 ×

D

4 X

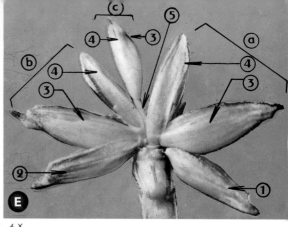

E

4 X

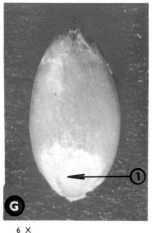

G

6 ×

H

6 ×

F

In observing head-on (photo D) one of the parts of the ear, you can see that it is formed of interlocked scales. Separate these scales (photo E); the first two (1 and 2) called glumes, envelop three small parts (a, b, c). Each of these consists of two scales (3 and 4) called lemma or flowering glume, in the middle of which is a flower. The part shown in photo D is therefore an inflorescence. This inflorescence contains 3 to 5 flowers which alternate all along a short axis (5): this is therefore a small ear, called a spikelet.

To study one of the flowers of the spikelet, (a) for example, turn it sideways, then pull out the glume (1) and lemma (3). With the palea (4) remaining in place, note (photo F) that the flower, borne by a short peduncle (1) comprises:

● 3 stamens, one of which is free. Their filaments are long and slender. When mature, their anthers have the shape of an X.

● A gynoecium of a single carpel. The globulous ovary (3), which contains a single ovule, is partly hidden by two small scales, the lodicules (2). It is surmounted by two feathery stigmas.

These flowers being without calyx or corolla, the glumes have a protective rôle.

The Fruit and the Seed

The stamens and the ovary are ripe before the flower opens and fertilization generally takes place in the still-closed flower. Therefore, in wheat, fertilization is direct.

However, when the glumes open, they free the stamens (photo C) whose anthers sway at the end of a long filament. The wind can thus carry the pollen, and it is possible that cross-pollination sometimes takes place.

46

After fertilization, the ovary develops and changes into a dry fruit that does not open, a caryopsis—this is the grain of wheat.

Study this grain, or if this is not possible, photos G, H and I. You will recognize:

● A curved side (photo G), the front face, whose base has a projecting part (1). This projection corresponds with the embryo (photo I).

● A flat side (photo H) with a deep groove.

● A tip furnished with hairs. Try to remove the seed of this fruit—it is impossible. This fruit is not therefore a true achene. Neither is it a seed: it is a fruit which resembles a seed.

Cut this fruit along the groove (photo I). You will see that it comprises:

● An envelope (1) which represents the closely fused pericarp of the fruit and testa of the seed. It is obvious why seed and fruit cannot be separated.

● Food reserves formed of a layer rich in gluten (2) and of a central part rich with starch, the endosperm (3). An embryo consisting of a plumule (4) enveloped in a kind of case (5) or coleoptile; a hypocotyl (6), a radicle (7), also enveloped in a case or colorhiza (8), and a scutellum (9). This single shield-shaped cotyledon is next to the food reserves.

As the embryo has only a single cotyledon, wheat is a monocotyledon.

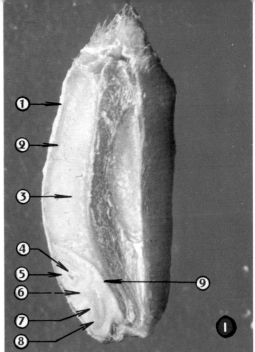

LIFE AND CULTIVATION OF WHEAT

The seeds are quick to germinate in damp, aerated and fertile soil.

By placing a few grains of wheat on damp absorbent cotton-wool, you can follow the first stages of this germination. Note that the plumule, whose development follows that of the roots (photo J), remains for a certain time enclosed in the coleoptile (1) which grows at the same time as the plumule. From this colorless case, the first leaves will later emerge.

In the soil, the little stem from the seed grows sideways. From its nodes appear adventitious roots and buds which produce secondary stems (tillers).

On these, adventitious roots and aerial roots will develop; numerous stems can thus form from one seed.

In summer, when the wheat has ripened, the stems dry up, the ears turn yellow (this is the time of harvesting), then the plant dies. Wheat is therefore an annual plant.

Conclusion

Wheat is a herbaceous, annual monocotyledon. Its stems are culms. Its leaves are ensheathed, with parallel veins. Its inflorescences are composed of spikelets. Its fruits resemble seeds. Wheat belongs to the family *Gramineae*, the family of grasses (from the Latin, *gramen*, turf).

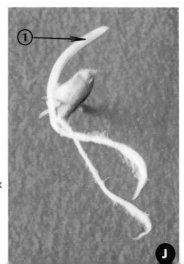

1.5 X

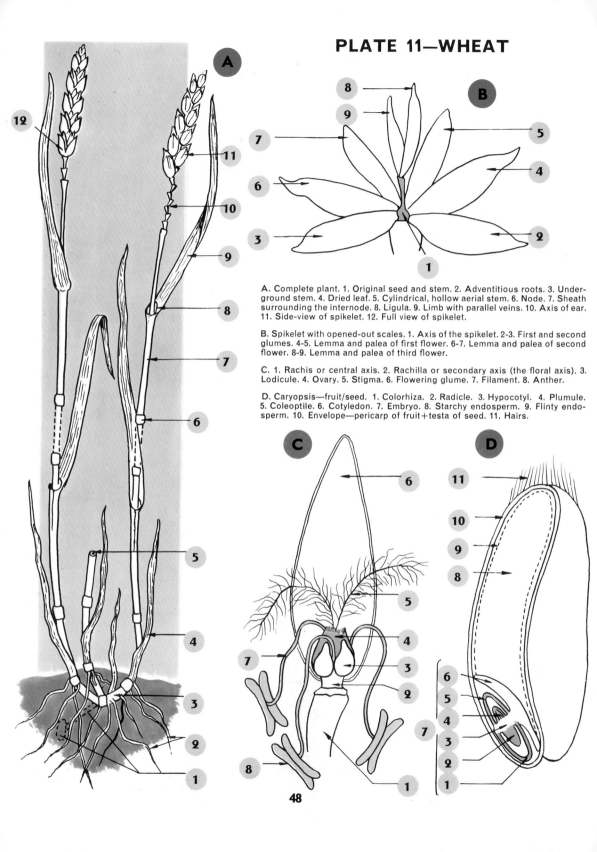

PLATE 11—WHEAT

A. Complete plant. 1. Original seed and stem. 2. Adventitious roots. 3. Underground stem. 4. Dried leaf. 5. Cylindrical, hollow aerial stem. 6. Node. 7. Sheath surrounding the internode. 8. Ligula. 9. Limb with parallel veins. 10. Axis of ear. 11. Side-view of spikelet. 12. Full view of spikelet.

B. Spikelet with opened-out scales. 1. Axis of the spikelet. 2-3. First and second glumes. 4-5. Lemma and palea of first flower. 6-7. Lemma and palea of second flower. 8-9. Lemma and palea of third flower.

C. 1. Rachis or central axis. 2. Rachilla or secondary axis (the floral axis). 3. Lodicule. 4. Ovary. 5. Stigma. 6. Flowering glume. 7. Filament. 8. Anther.

D. Caryopsis—fruit/seed. 1. Colorhiza. 2. Radicle. 3. Hypocotyl. 4. Plumule. 5. Coleoptile. 6. Cotyledon. 7. Embryo. 8. Starchy endosperm. 9. Flinty endosperm. 10. Envelope—pericarp of fruit+testa of seed. 11. Hairs.

48

× 1/3

× 1/3

× 1/3

SOME PLANTS OF THE FAMILY GRAMINEAE

All of this family, like wheat, have:

- A one-cotyledon seed.
- A culm-type stem, generally herbaceous.
- Ensheathed leaves with parallel veins.
- Inflorescences composed of spikelets.
- A fruit that looks like a seed.

This large family, with classification based on the nature of the spikelet, comprises:

Cereals or Gramineae Cultivated for their Seeds

- The wheats, some of which have their inferior glumellas lengthened by a spine.

× 1/3

- Oats (*Avena*, spp.) (photo A), whose spikelets form panicles, with long narrow glumes and a lemma bearing a long bristle (awn).
- Rye (*Secale*, spp.) (photo B), whose spikelets resemble those of wheat, are characterized by the long hairs (awns) of their lemmas. Their glumes are narrower than those of wheat.
- Barley (*Hordeum*, sp.) which differs from rye in that each plate of the ear's axis bears three spikelets.
- Maize (*Zea mays*), whose flowers are divided into male (tassels) and female (ears) flowers.

Fodder Gramineae

- Perennial rye grass (*Lolium perenne*) (photo C) whose spikelets are spaced out and in the same plane as the axis.
- Timothy or cats-tail (*Phleum pratense*) (photo D) whose ears, with tight spikes, are like pipe cleaners.

Commercial Gramineae

- Bamboo, whose woody stems are used to make fishing rods.
- Sugar cane (*Saccharum officinarum*), from the stalks of which we extract sugar.
- Esparto (*Stipa tenacissima*), cultivated, from which we make rope and paper.

THE ARUM

The arums are often found in damp under growth and the shady borders of ponds. They flower in the spring and attract numerous flies through their evil-smelling scent.

VEGETATIVE SYSTEM

In photo A, the spotted arum, cuckoopint (*Arum maculatum*), like the Jack-in-the-pulpit (*Arisaema atrorubens*), not yet in flower, you can see:

AN AERIAL PART, comprised of a single herbaceous stem which bears several leaves reduced to their sheath (1), and two or three spear-shaped simple leaves, often dotted with black spots. If chewed, the leaves leave a disagreeable sensation of burning in the mouth; the mucus of the tongue is injured by tiny, sharp crystals in the leaf cells. The stem ends in an axis bearing a large bract shaped like a pointed horn: the spathe.

AN UNDERGROUND PART (photo B) comprised of a white, fleshy organ, ending in a brown, dried-up part. This organ bears a large bud (1); this is an underground stem filled with food reserves: a rhizome. The rhizome also bears the aerial stem and numerous adventitious roots.

The Flowers

At first closed and pointed, the green horn softens and opens (photo C). It reveals a fleshy, red-brown organ, shaped like a club. If you open the swollen part of the spathe (photo D) you will see that the red club is borne on a stem on which you can see, from bottom to top:

● Large white balls, packed tightly against one another, and bearing a small granular swelling. Open them and you will find several ovules. Each white organ is therefore an ovary, or more correctly, a female flower reduced to an ovary of a single carpel.

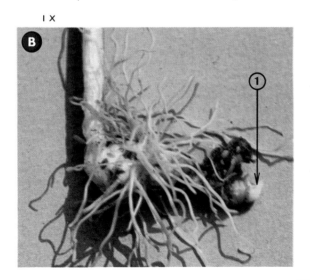

× 1/3

I ×

● Several female flowers whose ovary ends in a long filament (1); these are stunted, sterile flowers.

● At the end, brownish organs (2); these are compact anthers, with short filaments, which open through two longitudinal cracks. Each of these organs is therefore a male flower reduced to a single stamen.

● A crown of bristly hairs which reach the walls of the spathe. They correspond with the stunted male flowers.

This inflorescence therefore comprises incomplete male and female flowers grouped on an axis that ends in a club. This particular inflorescence is a spadix.

The Fruit and the Seed

If you should go for a walk during the early spring in an area of undergrowth where arums grow, you will encounter a great number of flies in the vicinity. You might also be struck by a disagreeable smell. The club of the spadix secretes a nauseating volatile substance which attracts certain species of flies. These flies, attempting to enter the spathe, edge in between the bristly hairs of the spadix; but they are thereby imprisoned, as the hairs, pointing towards the bottom (photo D) prevent them from getting out again. The flies, turning round and round inside the spathe, bump up against the carpels, and, if their hairs are covered with pollen from another arum, cause fertilization of the ovaries to take place.

Next, the stamens, which are not yet ripe, open one by one. The imprisoned flies become covered with pollen. Overnight, the hairs of the spadix wither (photo E). The flies can now take flight and go to another plant where again they will pollinate the carpels. The spotted arum is therefore a plant adapted to pollination by insects.

After fertilization, the leaves, spathe, and red club dry up and die. The fertilized ovaries develop and (photo F) form small, fleshy, bright reddish-orange fruits; these are berries. Each berry encloses several seeds in a single

C

X 1/2

I X

D

E 2.5 X

F 1.5 X

cotyledon: the spotted arum is a monocotyledon.

LIFE OF THE ARUMS

After dispersal of the fruits, the spadix disappears. The rhizome, emptied of its food reserves, dries up. Its terminal part, which has grown, survives the winter. The following spring, the bud it bears forms new aerial organs. The spotted arum is therefore a plant which is perennial through its rhizome.

The young rhizome develops a new underground stem equipped with a bud. This bud, in turn, will accumulate food reserves, thereby preparing for the third year's blossoming.

Conclusion

The spotted arum is a monocotyledon, perennial through its rhizome. It bears an inflorescence in the form of a spadix, with reduced male and female flowers, surrounded by a spathe. Its fruits are berries. The spotted arum belongs to the family *Araceae*.

(Caption for plate on opposite page)

A. Whole plant. 1. Underground stem, or rhizome, which fills up with food reserves after flowering. 2. Adventitious root. 3. First leaves reduced to their sheath. 4. Green spotted leaves. 5. Upper part of spadix. 6. Spathe. 7. Stem of past year whose reserves have helped the blossoming during current year. 8. Branch stem. 9. Dead stem from two years previous. 10. Sheath. 11. Petiole. 12. Spear-shaped leaf blade.

B. Inflorescence after partial section of the spathe. 1. Bract (spathe). 2. Axis of the inflorescence swollen into club (spadix). 3. Hairs (sterile male flowers). 4. Male flowers. 5. Stunted female flowers. 6. Female flowers.

C. Fruit. 1. Fruit (red berry). 2. Withered bract.
Fertilization cannot be direct, as the female flowers ripen before the male flowers. Transport of pollen is by flies.

PLATE 12—THE ARUM

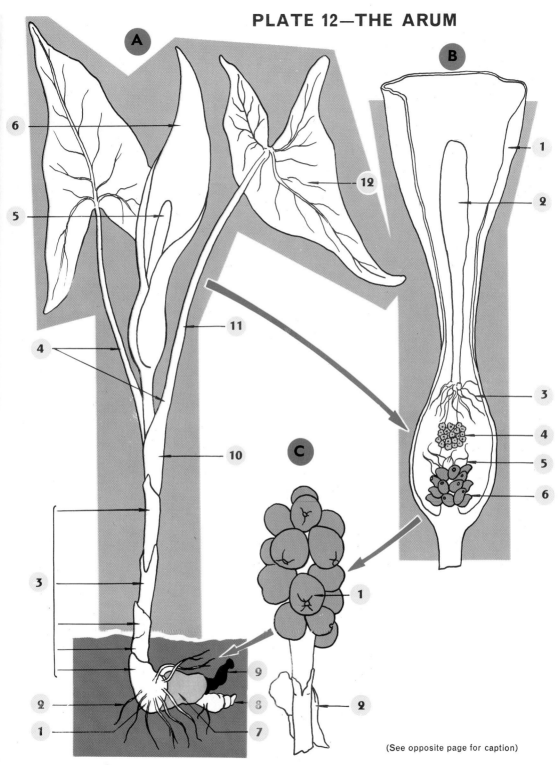

(See opposite page for caption)

THE PINE

X 1/100

The pine was formerly found in abundance in sandy regions, but large-scale lumbering and subsequent land cultivation have depleted its numbers. However, this tree may still be found in our forests as well as in arid places.

VEGETATIVE SYSTEM

The Scotch pine (*Pinus sylvestris*) (photo A) shows:

AN AERIAL PART, comprised of a straight, slender trunk, whose reddish-brown bark (photo B) is deeply cracked. The trunk, if injured, exudes through its bark a sticky, shiny liquid with a smell similar to that of turpentine or varnish: this liquid is resin. The resin, impermeable to water, makes the wood of the pine almost rot-proof and highly desirable as a weather-resistant timber.

Each of the pendant branches forms a broadly-spread bough. Short at the summit of the tree, long at its base, the branches give the crown its characteristic shape.

The leaves (photo D), long ($2\frac{3}{8}''$) and narrow, hard, leathery, needle-shaped, are grouped in twos and borne on a short branch which joins to the axils by a small scale. The leaves do not fall in winter: the pine has evergreen leaves.

AN UNDERGROUND PART formed of superficial roots (photo C) and of roots forced deeply into the ground. The main root is a long tap root. You will understand why the pine needs a thick layer of dry soil, light and aerated, to carry sufficient oxygen to the deep roots.

LIFE OF THE PINE

The end of each branch bears a bud protected by reddish-brown, resinous scales. In spring (photo D), these buds grow into young shoots, upright like tapers (1), and with soft green leaves. After four or five years, the leaves die and fall, forming on the ground a carpet of needles joined in pairs. In this way, the base of the branches becomes bare, while the ends grow.

X 1/6

REPRODUCTION

Study photo D. At the base of the young shoots you can see a heap of small, upright, yellowish-green cones formed of overlapping scales. In mid-spring (photo D) the scales open out from the axis that bears them and a fine yellow powder escapes from the cones. In the region of pine forests, this powder is carried long distances by wind and sometimes forms clouds of such magnitude that the name of "sulphur rain" has been given to them.

Examine a little of this powder through the microscope (photo E). It is made up of a multitude of small grains, each comprising a clear central part flanked by two dark lateral swellings: these are pollen grains. The dark swellings are hollow and form two small balloons which lighten each grain, adapting it for pollination by wind.

Remove a scale from a cone; on its lower side are two small sacs (the pollen sacs) from which the pollen runs. Each scale therefore is equivalent to a stamen and the yellow cones are male reproductive organs.

In photo D, at the top of a young shoot, is a small purplish-blue cone; you can see two, one of them sectioned lengthwise, in photo F. These two cones are also formed of scales fixed on an axis visible on the sectioned cone. Pull out a scale; on its upper face (photo G) you will see two small oval, whitish organs: these are ovules (1). The scale bearing them is equivalent to a carpel; the purplish-blue cones are female organs.

Note that, unlike the plants studied previously, the carpels of the pine are flat, they *do not form an ovary*, and in consequence the ovules are uncovered.

In late spring, the female cones and their ovules receive some of the pollen carried by the wind. Occasionally fertilization does not take place until a year after pollination, because the young ovules are not ripe, and fusion of the living matter of the ovule and of the pollen grain cannot take place.

After fertilization, the female cone increases slightly in volume and its scales thicken, leaving

55

C

× 1/50

× 1/5   D

120 ×   E

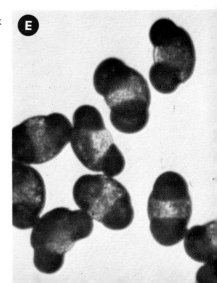

2 X

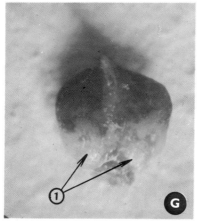

X 1/3   1,5 X

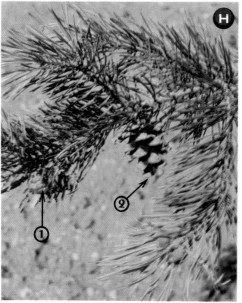

no space between them. The cone will pass its first winter in this form. In spring, it will renew its growth, changing its shape and height (photo H, 1). By autumn, it will have become a pine cone, woody and hard. It will thus pass a second winter, then in the following spring (two years after pollination), its scales will open out as a result of dryness (photo H, 2) and the seeds will be set free. After fertilization, the ovules will be changed into seeds containing an embryo surrounded by food reserves.

The seeds (photo I) will be furnished with a membranous wing which will allow the wind to carry them a distance. Each seed will afterwards germinate into a small plant (photo J) possessing 6 needle-shaped cotyledons. The pine cone, empty of its seeds, ends by falling on the ground.

Since the pine has pollen and ovules that become seeds, it can be classed, like the flowering plants previously studied, among seed-bearing plants, or spermatophytes (from two Greek words, meaning "seed" and "plant").

However, the plants previously studied, which have seeds enclosed in a fruit, are classed in the sub-branch of plants with enclosed seeds, or angiosperms (from two Greek words meaning "hidden" and "seed"), while the pine will be classed in the sub-branch of plants with naked seeds, or gymnosperms (from two Greek words: "naked" and "seed").

All the gymnosperms which, like the pine, have reproductive organs grouped in cones belong to the order of conifers.

Conclusion

The pine is a tree possessing roots, a trunk, evergreen leaves in the shape of needles, and reproductive organs grouped in male and female cones borne on the same tree. Its seeds are "naked." It belongs to the sub-branch of gymnosperms, to the order of conifers, and the family *Pinaceae*.

SOME PLANTS OF THE ORDER CONIFERAE

Whether trees or shrubs, plants in this order have leaves in the form of needles or scales, and reproductive organs grouped in unisexual cones.

PLATE 13—THE PINE

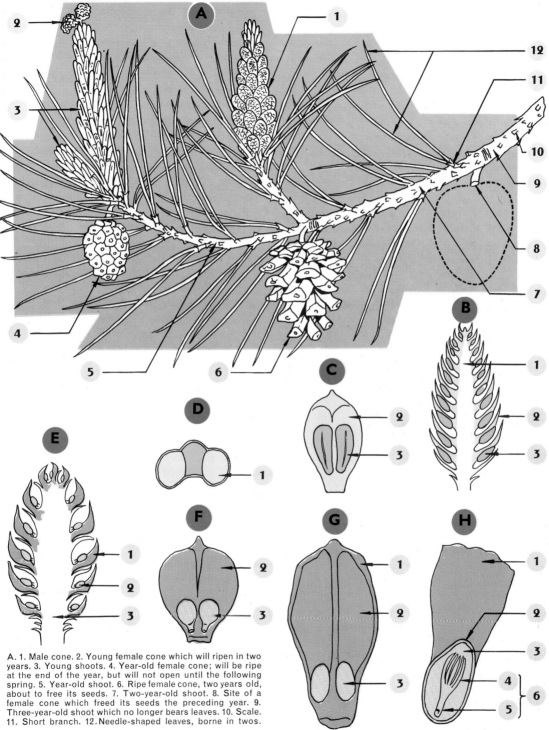

A. 1. Male cone. 2. Young female cone which will ripen in two years. 3. Young shoots. 4. Year-old female cone; will be ripe at the end of the year, but will not open until the following spring. 5. Year-old shoot. 6. Ripe female cone, two years old, about to free its seeds. 7. Two-year-old shoot. 8. Site of a female cone which freed its seeds the preceding year. 9. Three-year-old shoot which no longer bears leaves. 10. Scale. 11. Short branch. 12. Needle-shaped leaves, borne in twos.

B. Schematic section of the male cone. 1. Axis of cone. 2. Scale. 3. Pollen sac.

C. Scale of a male cone seen from its lower side. 2. Scale. 3. Pollen sac. D. Pollen grain with its small balloons (1). E. Schematic section of female cone. 1. Scale of cone. 2.

Naked seed. 3. Axis of cone. F. Scale of an immature female cone seen from its upper side. 2. Scale. 3. Seed. G. Scale of a mature female cone, viewed from its upper side. 1. Scale (carpel). 2. Wing. 3. Seed. H. Section of seed. 1. Wing. 2. Testa. 3. Endosperm (food store). 4. Cotyledons. 5. Radicle. 6. Plant embryo.

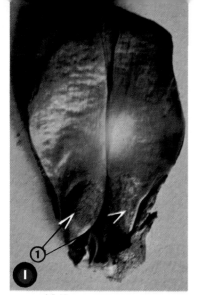

1.5 X

1 X

× 1/40

58

The Pinaceae

This family, including the pine, has needle leaves inserted in a spiral pattern; curved cones of which the scales of the female cones bear two ovules, and those of the male cones, two pollen sacs; pollen grains equipped with small "balloons"; examples being:

The Austrian or black pine (*P. nigra*), which differs from the Scotch and Norway pines in its leaves, which are longer (4") and darker.

The spruce (*Picea*, sp.), the traditional "Christmas tree." Its stiff, prickly leaves are attached, one by one, all around the branches. The female cones (photo A) are pendant, their scales tightly packed, and when they are ripe, they all fall on the ground.

The balsam fir (*Abies balsamea*), distinguishable from the spruce by its non-prickly flat leaves, which bear two white bands on their lower face, and by its upright cones which do not detach.

The larch (*Larix laricina* and *L. europaea*), the only common conifer to lose its needles in winter. Its needles (photo B) are supple, grouped in dense clumps on short branches. The small, round cones remain attached to the tree for many years.

The Cupressaceae

In this family, the leaves are often in the form of scales, and the cones are small:

Western red cedar (*Thuja occidentalis*) (photo D) whose scaly leaves grip tightly round the branches. The small cones terminate in several sterile scales.

× 3/4

X 1/2

D

X 1/2 E

The cypresses (*Chamaecyparis thyoides* or other species) (photo E) have leaves arranged like those of the Thuja. They have round cones, formed from a dozen scales, all attached at one point.

The juniper (*Juneripus communis*) (photo G) is recognized by its smell. Its very short branches completely mask the trunk. Its leaves are sharp-pointed needles, grouped 3 to a node. The female cones whose scales become fleshy and violet at maturity are wrongly called "berries."

The Taxaceae

The Yew (*Taxus baccata*) (page 3) which has a pinelike bearing, is characterized by ovules which are terminal, detached, and not protected by a scale. At maturity, its seeds are covered by a fleshy, red swelling called an aril.

The Gingko (*Gingko biloba*) (photo F) is of an order related to that of the conifers; except for the "dawn cypress" found in the interior of China, all other specimens of the order are fossils. Regarded in Asia as a sacred tree, the gingko was cultivated around Buddhist temples, and it is because of the care thus bestowed on it that it has survived to the present time.

X 1/2 G

X 1/3

F

4 X

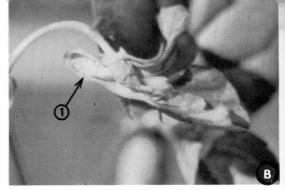

3 X

POLLINATION

For a flowering plant to be able to form fruits, its ovules must be fertilized—there must be fusion of the living matter of a pollen grain with that of an ovule. This fusion can only take place if the pollen is transported in some way to the stigmas of the carpels. It is essential that the fertilizing substance of the pollen (male gametes) make their way to the ovary and reach the ovules (female gametes). For fertilization and fruit formation to take place, pollination is essential.

SELF OR DIRECT POLLINATION

There is direct pollination when the pollen of a flower is carried to its own stigmas. This can be brought about by:

● Movement of the flowers caused either by wind or by insects.

● Movement of the stamens: The barberry,

for example, is a spiny shrub which flowers at the beginning of spring and has 6 stamens stretched around the ovary. What happens if you touch the filament of a stamen (photo A) in the way insects do? The stamens fall sharply on to the ovary. This movement throws pollen grain on to the stigma.

● The arrangement of the stamens in relation to the stigmas. In the nightshade family (*Solanaceae*), the hairy anthers of the 5 stamens form a collar around the style and open inwardly towards the stigma. Direct pollination also takes place in:

● Flowers which do not open, such as the violet (*Viola*, sp.). Next to the purplish flowers (photo B) familiar to you, there are small green flowers, always situated near the ground, which never open. Their corolla is reduced, and the male gametes from the pollen pass directly from the stamens to the ovary. It is these flowers which form the most numerous fruits.

● Plants with inaccessible reproductive organs. This unusual characteristic is found in the pea and the bean, as well as other papilionaceous plants where the carpel and stamens are entirely covered by the keel. Neither wind nor insects can reach them.

● Plants with organs which ripen before the flower opens. In wheat, barley, and oats, the pollen fertilizes the ovary of the flower even before it is open.

X 1/3

CROSS-POLLINATION

This takes place when pollen is carried to the stigmas of another flower of the same species. This event, by far the most frequent, always requires the intervention of a pollen-carrying agent. Cross-pollination can be brought about by:

Wind

We have already seen the wind's rôle in numerous plants, notably the pine; trees or shrubs with unisexual catkins, such as oak; the beech (photo C shows male catkins), the chestnut and the alder.

Apart from wheat, barley, and oats, this method of pollination is common to all the *Gramineae*. In these, the stamens hang outside the spikelets and their X-shaped anthers swing at the end of a long filament. The arrangement of the inflorescences at the end of long flexible stems again permits dispersion of the pollen. It is the long, feathery stigmas that catch it.

These characteristics can be most clearly seen in corn or maize (*Zea mays*). This graminaceous plant has male inflorescences (photo D) situated at the top of the stems, and, lower down, female inflorescences (photo E) from which long stigmas emerge out of an assembly of bracts surrounding the female organs.

All these plants and many others (spinach, sorrel, hop, etc.) possess common features:
- Absence of aroma and nectar.
- Reduced perianth.
- Numerous stamens, very apparent, with long filaments.

X 1/5

X 1/5

I X

X 1/2

61

× 1/4

× 1/2

× 1/2

- Abundant pollen, light and dry.
- Long, hairy, sticky stigmas.
- Growth together in dense patches (like forest trees and meadow plants).

As most of these characteristics encourage the action of the wind, these plants are said to be adapted to pollination by wind.

Insects

Look at the bumble-bee on a thistle (photo F) and the tortoise-shell butterfly gathering nectar from a burdock (photo G). In going from flower to flower, the insects become covered with pollen which they carry and deposit sooner or later on the stigmas of other flowers of the same species.

You know already what it is that attracts insects to flowers, namely:

THE PRESENCE OF NECTAR secreted by glands or hairs situated in various places in different plants: For instance, the nectar is at the back of the corolla in the foxglove (*Digitalis purpurea*) shown in photo H, the heather, the clover, and the dead nettle. It is at the base of the petals in the buttercup, in a swelling of the petals in the aconite or monkshood, in a hollow spur in the orchid, and again in the violet (photo B) where the spur (1) contains two nectar glands which are expansions of two ventral stamens. The nectar is at the base of the stamens or ovary in the umbellifers, the willow, and the maple. It is on the calyx in the pink and iris (photo J). In the iris, the sepals are turned up at the base and are covered with yellow hairs rich in nectar.

THE ABUNDANCE OF POLLEN, which is the food of wasps, bees and their larvae. Pollen is easily found in plants of the family *Rosaceae*, among which are numerous fruit trees. The rôle of insects in pollination is so important that fruit growers assure an abundant crop by placing bee-hives in their orchards. The buttercups and the willow also provide insects with pollen in abundance.

62

THE AROMA OF THE BLOSSOM, such as that of the hawthorn, the wild rose, the wallflower, the pink, the arum and the umbellifers.

THE COLORATION AND HEIGHT OF THE PERIANTH, as for example in the tulip and the buttercup and their families.

ANATOMICAL DEVICES that facilitate pollination, such as:

THE ARRANGEMENT OF THE NECTARY. In the iris, for example (photo J) the nectar-gathering insect rubs its back against the large anther (1) that surmounts the sepals. Upon flying to another flower, it deposits this pollen on the wide stigma (2) which is situated above each stamen.

MOVEMENTS. Take the case of the stamens of the barberry (photo A) or the bascule stamens of the sage. In relaxing, the stamen hits the insect and thus becomes covered by the pollen carried by the insect.

Special devices, like the pollen masses of orchids (photo T, page 67), and the arum (page 51) imprison the insects.

All plants which possess characteristics causing or facilitating the intervention of insects, are plants adapted to pollination by insects.

In certain plants, pollination depends on insects of one particular species. Such plants are:

THE HONEYSUCKLE (photo K) which is fertilized by nocturnal moths. Its whitish flower, clearly visible on an evening, opens out at twilight and attracts moths by its penetrating scent. Only the moth's long proboscis can draw nectar from the bottom of the corolla.

THE BORAGE (*Borago officinales*), whose petals bear ligulae (photo L), which close the corolla tightly. Only insects strong enough to open them, such as bumble-bees, can pollinate them.

THE VANILLA PLANT, an orchid originating in Mexico, which under natural conditions is only fertilized by a small wasp.

3 X

THE ARUM which is only fertilized by small flies.

Water

The pollen is carried by water to fertilize the flowers of certain aquatic plants. These have a reduced perianth, their pollen is light and abundant, and their stigmas are long and feathery, characteristics similar to those of plants pollinated by the wind.

Man

In the course of plant cultivation, man often takes the place of the natural pollination agent. For example, where the vanilla plant has been imported and cultivated, and the small pollinating wasp does not exist, man is compelled to pollinate by hand, replacing the head of the insect by a small bamboo stick. It is the same with the numerous hothouse orchids. If seeds are wanted, pollination must be effected artificially.

Artificial pollination also renders great services to agriculture. It makes it possible to create new varieties by crossing two strains of the same species. Thus numerous varieties of hybrid plants have been created.

PLATE 14—POLLINATION

A. Longitudinal section of the flower of the barberry. 1. Anther opening through pores. 2. Filament. 3. Stigma. 4. Ovary. 5. Calyx. 6. Corolla. Direct pollination is encouraged by movement of the stamens.

B. Longitudinal section of the flower of the violet. 1. Calyx. 2. Corolla. 3. Style. 4. Ovary. 5. Anther. 6. Nectariferous extension. 7. Spur. Cross-pollination is by insects attracted by the nectar.

Caption continued on opposite page.

The White Campion

2 X   2 X

The Mallow

3 X   3 X

Caption for opposite page

C and D. Longitudinal sections of sage flowers: C is male stage, D is female stage. 1. Calyx. 2. Corolla. 3. Connective. 4. Filament. 5. Anther. 6. Pointed stigma (female elements not yet ripe). 7. Divided stigma (ripe female elements). 8. Pollinating insect. 9. Style. 10. Ovary. 11. Wilted stamen. Cross-pollination is obligatory (the stamens are ripe before the carpels) and is made easy by the rocking movement of the stamens.

E. Longitudinal section of aristolochia flower. 1. Perianth. 2. Hairs. 3. Stamens. 4. Ovary. 5. Style. 6. Stigma. Cross-pollination is obligatory, as the carpels are ripe before the

stamens. The hairs hold prisoner the pollinating insect attracted by the scent.

F. Longitudinal section of the flower of the mallow at female stage. 1. Stigmas. 2. Style. 3. Ovary. 4. Calyx. 5. Corolla. 6. Wilted stamens. Cross-pollination is obligatory as the stamens are ripe before the carpels.

G. Longitudinal section of the flower of the iris. 1. Stigmas. 2. Styles. 3. Ovary. 4. Anther. 5. Calyx. 6. Hairs. 7. Corolla. Cross-pollination is obligatory as the pollen cannot fall on the stigmas.

3 X

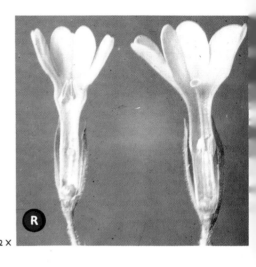

2 X

× 1/2

CONDITIONS OF CROSS-POLLINATION

It is obvious that cross-pollination is obligatory for all plants with unisexual flowers, whether these are on the same plant, as with the corn (maize) in photos D and E, or on different plants, as with the white campion (photos M and N). The latter plant has some stems bearing flowers that have only one ovary formed of 5 fused carpels. Other plants (photo N) bear only flowers with 10 stamens—the flowers open in the evening and pollination is by moths.

Further examples can be found among trees with catkins.

Cross-pollination is frequent in many plants having bi-sexual flowers. It is even obligatory for a certain number of plants which have:

Flowers Whose Stamens Are Ripe Before the Carpels

Look at the flowers of the mallow (*Malva sylvestris*) in photos O and P. Photo O shows a bush of stamens whose filaments are fused at the bottom into a tube. The upper anthers are ripe and liberate their pollen dust. The styles are not visible. Photo P, in contrast, shows wilted stamens, but red styles emerge from the flower. The stamens are therefore empty of pollen at the time the stigmas are ripe. Insects, attracted by the nectar, go from a young flower, at the male stage, to an older flower, at the female stage, and bring about pollination.

The same situation exists with the pink (photo S), the composites, such as the dandelion (photo B, page 40, showing the female stage), the umbellifers (the carrot shown in photo C, page 37, is at the female stage), the *Gramineae*, the columbine, the *Papilionaceae*, and the dead nettle.

Flowers Whose Carpels are Ripe Before the Stamens

This is the case with the arum, the belladonna and the aristolochia (photo Q), a climbing plant whose pollination is effected by flies. Its trap is a flower with an inferior ovary, and not an inflorescence like the arum. The large white mass that you see on this flower cut lengthwise is formed by the full-blown stigmas. Below, you can see the stamens that are not yet ripe.

Flowers Whose Stamens and Carpels Cannot Enter into Contact

THE PRIMROSE (*Primula vulgaris*) (photo R), which has two kinds of plants: One kind bearing flowers whose style is short and whose stamens are placed very high above the corolla, and the other kind having flowers with a long style and stamens at the bottom of the corolla. If you examine these two kinds of flowers, you will observe that the arrangement of the parts is such that only nectar-gathering insects can transport pollen from a flower with a long style to a flower with a short style and vice versa.

THE ORCHIDS (photo T) whose sticky pollen cannot fall on the stigma.

THE IRIS, whose styles and stigmas (photo J, 2) bend towards the exterior. The surface of the stigmas on which the pollen should fall is situated above the stamens, so direct transportation cannot take place.

30 X

Flowers Which Cannot Fertilize Themselves Through Their Own Pollen

Such is the case with the corn poppy and the pear tree, for example, whose pollen can only fertilize the ovules if it falls on the stigma of another flower.

Parthenogenesis

In some plants of the composite group, seed production occasionally takes place through parthenogenesis, the development of an embryo from an unpollinated ovule. This situation is rare in the higher plants, however.

Conclusion

Pollination is essential for the formation of fruits and seeds. It can be self or cross, cross-pollination being by far the most frequent. Each species is adapted either to be fertilized by its own pollen, or to be pollinated by a pollen-carrying agent. This transportation of pollen is most frequently brought about by insects or by wind.

Artificial pollination makes possible the creation of new botanical varieties.

I X

I X

DISPERSAL OF FRUITS

AND SEEDS

You have learned that after fertilization the ovary changes into a fruit, while the ovules change into seeds which will produce new plants. If these seeds develop at the foot of the mother plant, the young plants will often die through lack of sun and food. The adult plant covers them with its shadow and draws nutritive elements from the soil.

If the fruits or seeds are carried far, the young plants grow more successfully, as they develop in an unexploited environment. Dispersal of fruits and seeds is therefore an essential factor in the multiplication and propagation of the species.

There are dry fruits and fleshy fruits, fruits that open and others that do not. Each has a different method of dispersal.

FRUITS THAT DO NOT OPEN

These are always dispersed whole, either by the plant itself which projects them by active dispersal or by various agents or by passive dispersal.

Active or Self Dispersal

This often takes place through an "explosion," as with the *Geraniaceae*, such as the

stork's-bill, also known as alfileria or pinclover (*Erodium cicutarium*) shown in photo A, whose superior ovary is formed of 5 fused carpels. At maturity, and if the weather is dry, the 5 fused carpels separate from one another, the style stands out in 5 strips which coil and

X 1/4

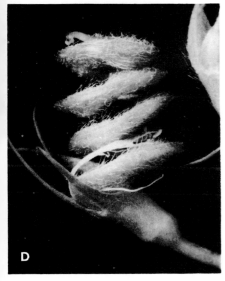

D

7 X

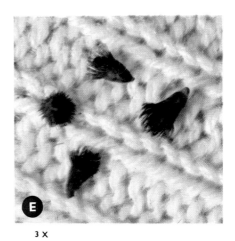

E

3 X

This pod, which contains only one seed, coils into a spiral in the process of drying.

● The mericarp of the carrot and of certain umbellifers which bristle with curved points. These fruits can be set together:

● The achene of the agrimony (*Agrimonia eupatoria*) (photo E), which is enclosed in a calyx whose hooked hairs cling just as easily

spring away from the middle part of the style which bears them. Through this fairly sharp movement, each strip throws an achene some distance from the mother plant.

Passive Dispersal

This can take place by means of:

THE WIND. Fruits distributed by the wind are usually carried on a long stalk, as in the dandelion (page 40), or are pendant, as in the maple. They are, in addition, dry, light and often winged or feathery. Thus there are:

● Winged fruits: a samara in the case of the elm (photo B) or a di-samara as in the maple (photo E, page 22). (In the case of the birch, the wing is formed by the bracts of the inflorescence.)

● Parachute fruits in the dandelion and the thistle (photo C) where the pappus is formed by the persistent hairs of the calyx.

BY ANIMALS. The fruits that cling to the hairs of animals and those fruits eaten or stored by animals.

Hooked fruits. Among the best known are:

● The pod of the lucerne (*Medicago sativa*) (photo D) which is furnished with small hooks.

F

I X

× 1/3

2 ×

I ×

to the woolly coverings of animals as they do to our clothes.

● The flower-heads of the burdock (*Arctium minus*) (photo F), probably well known to you because you have thrown them on the clothes of your friends. Here, the whole flower head fixes itself by means of its hooked bracts (1) and releases the smooth achenes (2) contained inside it.

● The awns of certain *Gramineae*, rye, barley, sterile brome-grass, whose beards stick easily into the fabric of our clothes.

Edible fruits—Among these are:

● Dry fruits rich in food stores. These include the beech nuts, hazel nuts, acorns and chestnuts, sought by squirrels. These rodents lose nuts in moving them and often forget where they have hidden their winter stores. The following spring, these fruits germinate far from their mother tree.

● Fleshy fruits. Berries like tomatoes and grapes, drupes like cherries and plums, fruits resembling berries such as the myrtle, currant and the gooseberry, and many other fruits that are juicy, scented, sweet and often of bright hues that attract animals. Their stones and pips, if swallowed, are not digested; they are found in their excreta where they germinate. Thrushes are very partial to the red berries of the chokeberry (*Pyrus arbutifolia*) (photo G), and, in eating them, ensure its propagation.

(NOTE: In the case of certain fruits like the strawberry and the fig, it is the achenes which pass through the digestive system without injury.)

WATER. In some instances, water can transport whole fruits. The coconut, fruit of the coconut palm, is water-tight and light; it floats on water and it is this mode of distribution that makes the coconut so abundant throughout the shores of the Pacific. In the case of the waterlily, the berries which detach themselves from the plant are carried by the water and eventually decay, thereby freeing their seeds a long way from the plant that bore them.

70

I X

X 1/5

FRUITS THAT OPEN

These fruits, generally dry, remain attached to the plant. They open to free the seeds which are then distributed.

Remember, these fruits can open in different ways:

● Through cracks, such as with the marsh marigold (*Caltha palustris*), the wallflower, and the tulip.

● Through holes, as in the capsule of the red poppy (*Papaver rhoeas*) (photo H). These holes are situated under a kind of roof formed by the fused stigmas, and the seeds are shaken out.

● By a serrated tear as in the primula and the pink.

● A circular tear as in the capsule of the scarlet pimpernel (*Anagallis arvensis*). Whatever the method of opening, distribution of the seeds can be active or passive.

Active Distribution

It is linked to a more or less explosive movement of the walls of the fruit. In this category are:

● The pods of many papilionaceous plants such as the bean and pea, which open in dry weather. The pods twist sharply, pressing on the seeds, which they project some distance.

● The capsules. In the jewelweed (balsam) (*Impatiens*, sp.) (photo I), when the capsule is ripe the slightest touch will cause it to burst, and this opening is accompanied by a twisting of the valves which scatters the seeds. See Plate 15.

I X

71

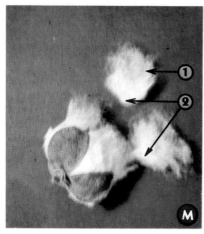

X 1/2

long hairs (1) of the seeds (2) which constitute the cotton used as a textile fibre.

- Winged seeds, like those of the pine.
- Small, light seeds, like those of the red poppy, the pink, the heather and the orchids.

ANIMALS. Seeds that are tasty or attractive draw principally birds and certain insects.

Thus, in the violet, the seeds have fleshy growths containing a liquid similar to nectar. Ants carry off these seeds in order to suck the sweet liquid, then they abandon them, thereby ensuring dispersal.

The large seed of the yew (page 3) is enclosed in a sweet, red mass, which attracts birds. The birds eat the entire seed and it is passed out with their droppings.

WATER. This is the method of transportation in the case of many plants that live at the edge of streams and ponds. The water iris for example, has seeds whose testa is waxy and waterproof, which allows the seeds to float and to be carried away by the current.

In rushes (photo N), which grow in damp ground, the capsule only opens when it rains,

In the violet and pansy (photo J), the capsule opens, then, through dryness, the edges of each valve draw together, pressing on the seeds which are ejected, in the manner of an orange pip that you can project by squeezing it between your fingers.

- Certain berries. In the squirting cucumber (*Echinocystis lobata*) (Plate 15) the fruit resembles a gherkin. At maturity, it is swollen with a juicy pulp which surrounds the seeds. The slightest touch causes the fruit to detach itself from the stalk, and the pressure of the walls on the pulp is such that the pulp and seeds are violently expelled as the fruit is jet propelled away from the plant.

Passive Distribution

This takes place through:

THE WIND. In this case, the fruit is generally borne by a long stalk and the seeds have characteristics which aid their transport; these, for example, are:

- Hairy seeds, like those of the willow-herb or fireweed (*Epilobium angustifolium*) (photos K and L), the willow, the poplar, and the cotton plant (photo M). In the last-named, it is the

X 1/8

PLATE 15

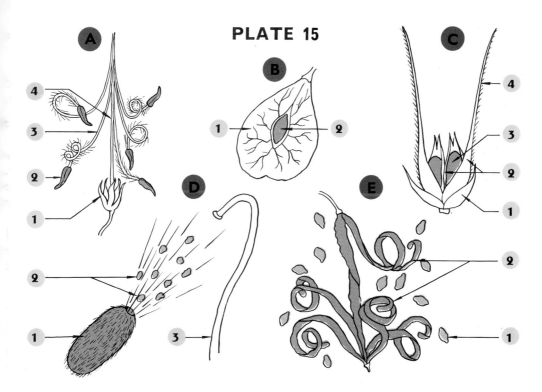

A. Fruits of the stork's-bill, active distribution. 1. Calyx. 2. Achene. 3. Coiled strip (style). 4. Axis (style).

B. Samara of elm, passive distribution by the wind. 1. Wing. 2. Achene.

C. Rye, passive dissemination by animals. 1. Glume. 2. Palea. 3. Fruit seed. 4. Beard bristling with teeth.

D. Dehiscence of the fruit of the squirting cucumber, active distribution of the seeds. 1. Fruit (berry). 2. Seeds. 3. Peduncle to which the fruit is attached.

E. Dehiscence of the fruit of the jewelweed (balsam), active distribution of the seeds. 1. Seed. 2. Valves of the fruit which coil up abruptly.

and the seeds are distributed by the running water. When the rushes are flattened by sudden showers, the seeds may germinate in the capsule and it is the small plants that are then disseminated.

MAN. Through his many cultivations of the soil, both useful or ornamental, man has voluntarily introduced many species into the flora of each country. In this way, tobacco, maize, the tomato and the potato, came from South America. The cauliflower, endive, cherry and peach came from Asia.

Conclusion

Distribution of fruits and seeds is essential to the propagation of species. This distribution can be active if the plant itself assures it, or passive if carried out by the wind, animals, water or man. Distribution by the wind is by far the most effective.

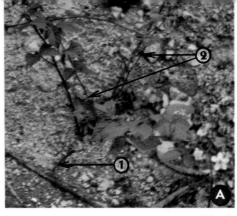

× 1/10   × 1/6

VEGETATIVE PROPAGATION

You have learned that many plants are able to produce new individuals through such organs as roots, stems and leaves. This is through a type of reproduction, very different from sexual reproduction, called vegetative propagation. You will see that man has exploited this in order to assure the propagation of many cultivated plants.

NATURAL VEGETATIVE PROPAGATION

This has various aspects, and can be brought about by different organs.

Stems

According to the circumstances, these are:

● Creeping stems. Thus, the stems of the pink easily form adventitious roots from the nodes, and if the base of the stem dies the rooted branch will produce a new plant.

In the blackberry (photo A), the end of the shoot (1) forces itself in the ground and forms

1 ×

C

adventitious roots. During the following year the buried terminal bud produces new aerial branches (2) which in turn root themselves by their ends. By this method, called natural layering, the blackberry quickly overruns large areas.

● Runners or stolons. You know about the strawberry (page 28), but the English or sweet violet (*Viola odorata*) and the creeping buttercup (*Ranunculus repens*) also form runners. Stems with very long internodes trail on the ground away from the mother plant. From certain nodes a new plant grows, quickly able to live by itself.

● Rhizomes. This type of propagation is found especially in plants having a branched rhizome like the iris (photo B) and the dead nettle. Rhizomes always bear buds at the nodes. If the rhizome is cut accidentally or if a part dies, each one (1) will produce a new plant. From this you can understand why these plants are usually found in clumps.

● Tubers. In the case of the potato (page 29), each "eye" of the tuber is able to form a new plant: it is enough to plant a piece of the tuber bearing an eye.

● Bulbs. In the tulip (page 13) a replacement bulb forms while the old bulb dies. This new bulb is often accompanied by a large number of smaller bulbs, called off-set bulbs or cloves, which also form new plants. In the garlic (photo C) these cloves are all equally developed. The lily, hyacinth, and the onion also form cloves.

● Suckers. The raspberry (photo F), and certain trees such as the poplar and plum, have stems that grow in the ground (1) and bear buds. From these buds develop shoots, called suckers (2) which afterwards separate from the mother plant.

Buds

This is found in the *Ranunculus*, the lesser celandine (*R. ficaria*) (photo D) which flowers in the spring in undergrowth, and whose flowers rarely form fruits, their pollen being sterile.

At the axils of the leaves (photo E), small white balls form, and these, falling on the ground, give birth to a plant. These small balls are called bulblets (1), but a microscopic examination shows that the white mass is not a bulb but a root swollen with food reserves. It bears the bud which will form the stem and leaves.

Roots

A number of plants have fleshy roots. The lesser celandine has many swollen roots, filled with stored food, which can separate and thus form several plants. It is the same with the dahlia (photo H), each of whose fleshy "rootlets" will give rise to a new plant.

Leaves

The *Bryophyllum*, sp. (photo G), is a thick-leaved ornamental plant on whose leaves plantlets develop (1). As soon as these have two small leaves and roots, they fall on the ground at the slightest shock and take root.

PROPAGATION OF CULTIVATED PLANTS

Plants developed from seeds often have important variations in comparison with their parents. Thus, without special precautions, the seeds of a four-o'clock (or Clarkia) with red flowers which have been fertilized by the pollen

D

I X

E (1)

X 1/2

X 1/8

F

(2)

(1)

PLATE 16

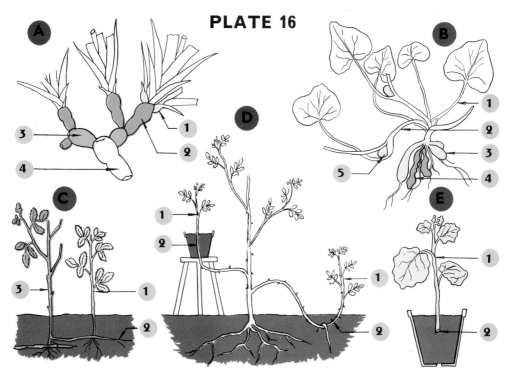

A. Branched or spreading rhizome of iris. 1. Current year's rhizome which will produce a flower-bearing stem. 2. Two-year-old rhizome which produces a flower-bearing stem. 3. Three-year-old rhizome. 4. Four-year-old rhizome.

B. Lesser Celandine. 1. Leaf. 2. Stem. 3. Current year's tuberous root which will produce a new plant in a year's time. 4. Year-old tuberous root, empty of its stored food. 5. Bulblet.

C. Raspberry. 1. This year's sucker. 2. Suckering stem that produced 1. 3. Year-old sucker that produced stem 2.

D. Two methods of layering a rose tree. 1. Layered branches. 2. Area where adventitious roots will form.

E. Geranium cutting. 1. This year's ripe shoot. 2. Point where roots will develop.

of a four-o'clock with white flowers will produce plants with pink flowers. Again, if you sow some tulip seeds, the young plants remain fragile for a long time, and it will be several years before they flower. Similarly, if you sow potato seeds, you will only obtain small tubers. On the contrary, the plants produced by vegetative propagation are absolutely identical, so man uses various procedures to help or cause this method of propagation, such as:

● Division of root stocks, with such plants as the iris (A, Plate 16), the dahlia (photo H) and the pink. These only require separation of the various parts.

● Layering. Bend a wild-rose branch and bury part of the stem (D, Plate 16). The buried nodes will produce adventitious roots; after this, it is only necessary to separate the branch

from the mother plant to have a new plant: this is layering. Such rooting of the branches of the blackberry is an instance of natural layering.

Note that, in the case of a plant with upright branches, it is sometimes necessary to surround the branch with a pot cut longitudinally and filled with earth—air-layering (D, Plate 16).

Layering applies to all the plants which easily form roots (raspberry, gooseberry, rose).

● Cuttings. At the end of summer, ripe geranium shoots are cut off, and then put in soil. They take root and thereby produce a new plant: a cutting has been made (E, Plate 16).

The privet (photo I), ivy and the willow, are examples of plants propagated by cuttings of stems. Since the cut stem cannot replace the water lost until roots are formed, the leaves

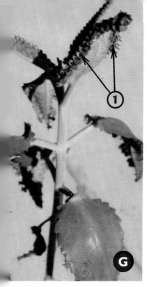

G

× 1/2

are partly or completely thinned out, so as to avoid excess water loss through transpiration.

Sometimes one can make cuttings from leaves. For example, if you bury the leaf stalk of an African violet leaf (photo J) numerous adventitious buds, which will produce new plants, form at the base.

● Grafting, used principally for propagation of roses and fruit trees. This operation consists of fixing on a strong growing plant of poor quality (the stock), a branch or a bud taken from another plant that you wish to propagate (the scion), because of the quality of its flowers or of its fruits. In this way a rose is grafted on a wild rose, and a pear on a wild quince.

To obtain a perfect union (graft) of the tissues of the subject to be reproduced (the scion) with those of the supporting plant (the stock) they are put in contact over a large surface of meristematic tissue (cambium). This operation is usually carried out at the beginning of spring, at the time when the sap begins to rise again. The main methods of grafting are:

● The cleft graft (photo K), used for fruit trees. The graft, a shoot whose base is cut in a wedge, is introduced into a slit made in the stem of the stock.

● The bud graft (photo L) used for rose trees. The graft bud, consisting of a bud and the adjoining bark, is introduced into a T-shaped cut made on the stock.

In every case, a tie (photo K) is made, to ensure close contact of the tissues, and the cut is coated with protective grafting wax or clay.

Conclusion

Vegetative propagation can take place naturally through various organs; roots, stems, buds and leaves. It can be encouraged or caused by various procedures: division, layering, cuttings, grafting. It assures rapid propagation of certain plants and preservation of the characteristics of the original stock.

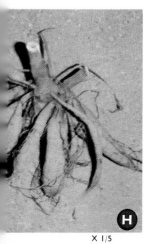

H

× 1/5
× 1/5

I

J

× 1/2

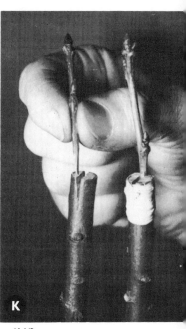

K

× 1/2
I ×

L

FERNS

The first fern we will study, called the rock polypody fern (*Polypodium virginianum*, var. *vulgare*) grows on old walls, among rocks, in shadowy, slightly humid places. It is a small, fairly common plant.

VEGETATIVE SYSTEM

On a carefully uprooted plant (photo A) you will distinguish:

AN AERIAL PART, consisting solely of leaves characterized by a long leaf stalk and a limb frond cut into numerous pinnae (1). These pinnae are covered by veins, which are the sap-conducting vessels. The young leaves are curled up into a crook.

AN UNDERGROUND PART, comprised of a brown organ, covered with scales, which creeps along close to the ground. The leaves join this underground stem separately. You know that such a stem is called a rhizome, and that the roots it bears are adventitious roots.

LIFE OF THE PLANT

The leaves, rhizome and roots persist during the winter. In the spring, the rhizome grows at one of its ends, the clearer end, where you can recognize a bud (2). New leaves then appear on the young parts of the rhizome, at the same time that the old parts die.

The fern is a perennial plant through its rhizome.

REPRODUCTION

On the lower side of the newly formed leaves you will observe small green "buttons" which will change into the brown bodies called sori visible on photo A. Through the magnifying-glass (photo B), each body appears formed of a group of small spheres.

Remove several of these spheres and study them through the microscope (photo C). Each sphere is formed of a globular sac carried on a small peduncle (1), and each sac is equipped with a brown arch, the indusium (2) resembling a toothed wheel. Examine an open sac; you will easily see that its opening is caused by contraction of the indusium. This opening,

which takes place through dryness, results in the liberation of the small "seeds" contained in the sacs. These "seeds" are called spores, and the sac is called a spore sac, or sporangium. The brown bodies situated under the leaves are therefore groups of sporangia.

The spores germinate on contact with damp soil. Each spore produces (photo D) a small green lamina whose lower side bears absorbent hairs (1). On completing its growth (photo E), this lamina measures about 1 cm. in diameter. This plant is different from the mother fern and is called a prothallus (from two Greek words meaning "before" and "branch").

The lower side of a prothallus through a microscope, shows small, spherical sacs in the middle part, and better still, on the edges (photo F). If you place the prothallus in water, you will see that certain sacs open and liberate a large number of small elements which move by revolving at great speed.

Photo G shows, greatly enlarged, one of these elements after coloration with iodine solution. It appears in the shape of a spiral mass equipped with long locomotory hairs: this element is a male or sperm cell. The three sacs shown in photo F are therefore antheridia.

On the same prothallus, in the vicinity of the notch (photo H), you can see flask-shaped organs called archegonia. These comprise:

● A large part, the venter or "ovary" (1), the middle of which is filled by a voluminous, dark cell: this is a female cell or "ovule" (2).

● A slightly smaller part, the neck (3), lined by a canal (4).

The organs of photo H are therefore sacs with female sex cells.

Swimming in the film of moisture that bathes the prothallus, the male cells swim towards the sacs containing the female cells. The male cell penetrates the canal, in order to fertilize the female cell. Several female organs will be fertilized on the same prothallus, but only one embryo will develop.

Look at the detached prothallus shown in photo I: it bears a young fern, already well developed. This fern is still firmly attached to

79

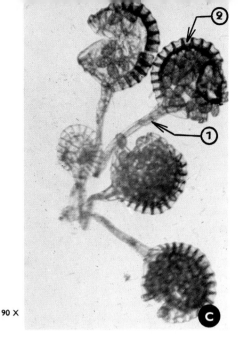

90 X   C

the prothallus, because at the beginning of its development it secured nourishment through this agency. Note, from photo J of a young plant cut along its axis, in addition to the first leaf (1) and the first root (3), the foot (2) which attaches itself to the prothallus (4). When the young fern is able to feed itself, the prothallus dies.

Reproduction of the polypody fern is therefore characterized by the alternation of generations: the fern proper derives from a fertilized female cell, producing spores (the sporophyte), and the prothallus, born of a spore produces male and female sex cells (the gametophytes).

Conclusion

The polypody fern is a perennial plant, having roots, a stem, leaves, and vessels. Its development is characterized by the alternation of

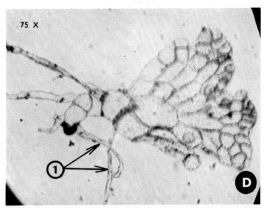

75 X   D

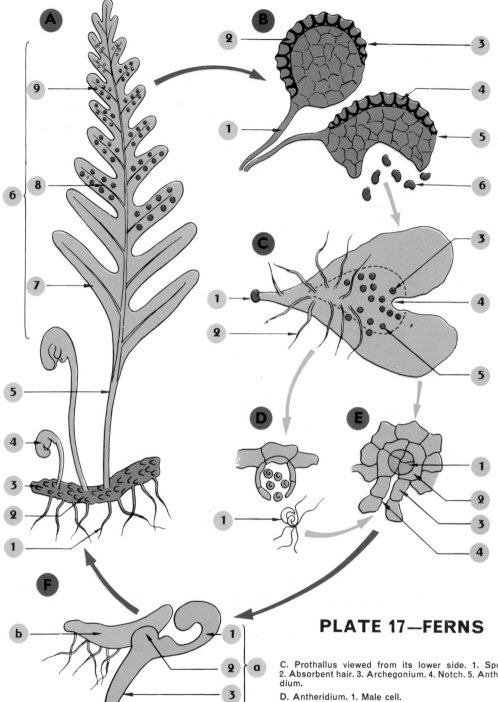

PLATE 17—FERNS

A. Complete rock polypody. 1. Adventitious roots. 2. Rhizome. 3. Bud. 4. Young curled leaf. 5. Petiole. 6. Frond. 7. Pinna. 8. Vein. 9. Sorus.

B. Sporangia of sorus viewed through microscope. 1. Stalk or sporangiophore. 2. Indusium. 3. Sporangium shut. 4. Indusium contracted. 5. Sporangium open. 6. Spore.

C. Prothallus viewed from its lower side. 1. Spore. 2. Absorbent hair. 3. Archegonium. 4. Notch. 5. Antheridium.

D. Antheridium. 1. Male cell.

E. Archegonium. 1. Female cell. 2. Venter. 3. Neck. 4. Canal.

F. Section showing the connection between the young plant (a) and the prothallus (b). 1. First leaf. 2. Foot. 3. First root.

The arrows correspond to the alternation between the plant proper (red arrows) and the prothallus (blue arrows).

different generations, a gametophyte generation giving rise to a sporophyte generation which in turn produces the next gametophyte, etc.

- The plant proper, born of a fertilized female cell, and producing spores.
- The prothallus, born of a spore, and producing male and female cells.

The polypody belongs to the class of ferns, and to the sub-kingdom of *Pteridophyta* (from two Greek words meaning "fern" and "plant").

SOME PLANTS OF THE SUB-KINGDOM OF PTERIDOPHYTA

Plants included in this sub-kingdom of 3 classes have a varied appearance, but all, like the rock polypody fern, are plants equipped with roots, a stem, leaves and sap-carrying ducts; plants whose female organs are flask-shaped, and whose reproduction is characterized by the succession of leafy, spore-producing plants, and prothalli which produce the male and female cells.

Class of Ferns

This class groups together plants whose young fronds are always rolled up into a crook.

- Hart's-tongue fern (*Phyllitis scolopendrium*). This fern, which likes dampness, is most abundant near wells and springs. It is distinguished by its long, complete leaves, reminiscent of a tongue, hence the name. The arrangement of sporangia, to which this plant owes its name, has been compared to that of the feet of a centipede.
- The Venus hair fern (*Adiantum capillusveneris*). This little fern generally grows on damp, shadowy walls. Its fronds have a black, rigid petiole, which bears pinnae separated and rounded at the summit. When the pinnae fall, the petioles look like tufts of hair, hence their name.
- The royal fern (*Osmunda regalis*). This is very common in siliceous soils, in sunlit glades. Its leaves, with very jagged fronds, often grow to 6½ feet above the ground, supported by a strong petiole. The sporangia are situated on the edge of the lobes and are protected by a fold

81

E

X 6

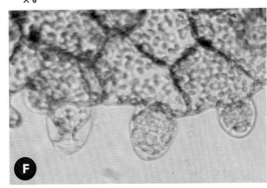

F

X 400

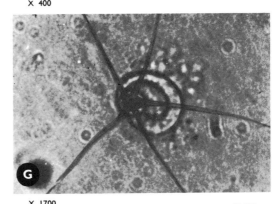

G

X 1700   X 350

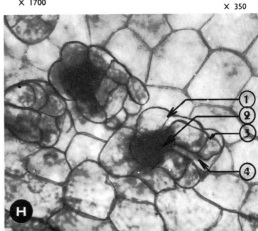

H

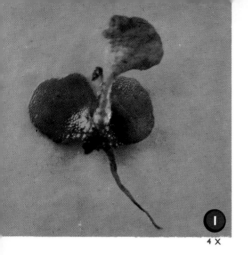

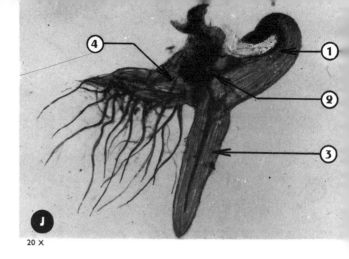

4 X

20 X

of the lobes. This is the largest fern of temperate regions, but in tropical regions may grow 50 feet tall. These ferns resemble palm trees.

Class of Horsetails

Horsetails (photo K) grow in damp places and their ribbed, hollow stems disjoint easily. The small leaves form collarettes on a level with the nodes. The stems which appear in spring have the ends swollen into a sporangia-bearing ear. The spores, which look like green powder, are interesting to observe through the microscope. They are equipped with four arms which roll up or unroll around them according to the

humidity of the air. The breath of the observer is sufficient to cause these movements.

Stems that appear at the end of spring (1) bear crowns of branches with the structure of stems on the level of their nodes. These are sterile stems.

Class of Lycopodia, the Club Mosses

This class comprises small plants (photo L) with slender, branching stems which bear small leaves. The stems creep and only the ends are upright. At the tip of the branches the leaves close up and form sporangia-bearing ears.

X 1/2

X 1/2

3 X

MOSSES

The cord moss (photo A) is a small weed plant, found anywhere that is at all suitable to vegetation. Cinder heaps and burnt fields are preferred locations. In such places cord moss, *Funaria hygrometrica*, may form a continuous mat several yards square. The only place it seems to avoid is strongly acid soil.

VEGETATIVE SYSTEM

Isolate a plant carefully, as has been done in photo B. You can observe that these plants consist of:
● A short stem bearing small green leaves.
● Fine, short hairs that run from the base of the stem: it has no roots.

In addition, the stem and the leaves are very different from the stems and leaves of the pteridophytes and spermatophytes as examination will reveal. The cord moss has no sap-conducting vessels and is therefore a moss.

LIFE OF THE PLANT

In wet weather, the cord moss forms attractive green carpets on the ground, but in dry weather it is not noticeable because it dries up and appears to be dead. Should some rain fall, however, it turns green again, absorbing water over the whole surface of its organs, and resumes its activity. It can be concluded that the cord moss needs water to live, but is very resistant to dryness. Its resistance to cold is equally remarkable.

This resistance to dryness, associated with the presence of chlorophyll, explains why certain mosses can grow in relatively arid surroundings.

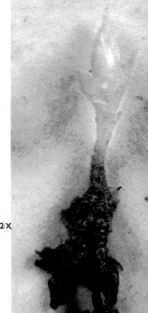

12 X

C

6 X

REPRODUCTION

Careful observation reveals that the plants are not identical. The leaves of certain plants (photo C) open into a rosette, in the middle of which you can see a small reddish bud. Photo D shows one of these plants detached.

With the tip of a scalpel, remove a piece of this bud and look at it through a microscope. You will be able to identify (photo E) green hairs (1), and brown club-shaped hairs (2).

These brown hairs, in opening, set free small, spiral-shaped elements (E, Plate 18), mobile because they bear two cilia: these are male sperm cells.

The hairs observed are therefore antheridia and the plants shown in photos C and D are male plants.

Study of other plants is more difficult, as their height does not exceed 1/10th of an inch at the start of their development. If you remove the leaves of these plants and examine their tips through the microscope you will see (photo F) hairs and kinds of small flasks comprising:

• A long narrow part, the neck (1) cut by a canal.

• A swollen part (2), containing a voluminous cell (3): this is a female cell.

The small flasks shown in photo F are therefore archegonia; and the plant shown in photo B is a female plant.

In rainy weather, the sacs with male cells open. The male cells swim in the water that covers the mosses and make their way to a female plant. A male sperm cell, penetrating

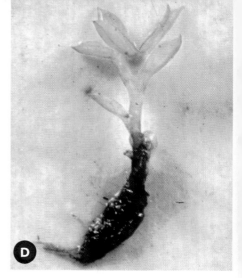

D

8 X

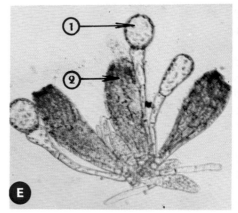

① ②

E

100 X

120 X

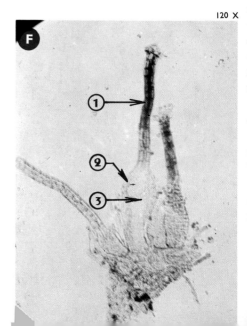

F

① ② ③

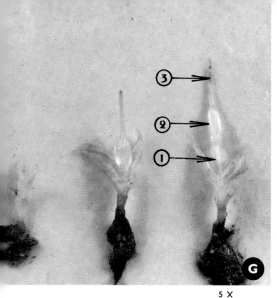

G 5 X

H 3 X

the neck canal, goes to unite with the female sex cell which will thus be fertilized.

Study photos G, H, I, J, which show the different phases of development of the embryo resulting from this fertilization. It is apparent that the embryo accomplishes its development on the female plant from which it draws its nourishment.

By looking at the plants shown in photo G— the plants from which several leaves have been removed—you can observe that:

● The embryo and the sac containing it grow at the same time.

● Its growth continuing, the organism divides into a narrow part, the bristle (1), and a swollen part, the capsule (2). The upper part of the sac covers the capsule with a kind of cap, the calyptra (3). You can see (photo H) that the bristle at first grows more quickly than the capsule.

Growth completed, the plant is at the stage shown in photo I, where you can distinguish:

● The long bristle (1), which twists as a result of dryness; hence the species name "hygrometric" is given to this moss.

● The capsule (3), closed by a small lid called an operculum (2), is covered by a calyptra (4).

At maturity, first the calyptra, then the operculum, fall (photo J). A brown powder

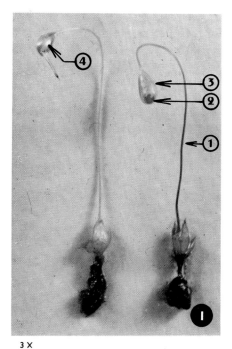

I 3 X

6 X

J

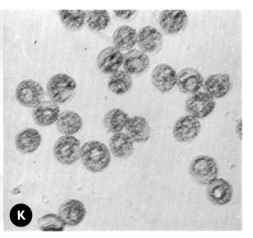

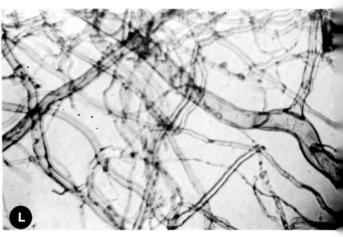

escapes from the dentated orifice (1). Microscopic examination (photo K) reveals that this powder is composed of small cells called spores. The organism "born" of the embryo therefore produces spores; it is called a sporophyte.

On damp ground the spores germinate and produce branching filaments (photo L) on which new moss plants will develop. This branching structure is called a protonema from which develops the next gametophyte generation.

Conclusion

The moss is a plant without vessels or roots. It has flask-shaped female organs. Its growth is characterized by the succession of two kinds of organisms:

● The plant proper, "born" of a spore, and producing male or female cells.

● The sporophyte, "born" of a fertilized female cell, and producing spores.

It belongs to the class of mosses and the sub-kingdom of *Bryophyta* (from two Greek words meaning "moss" and "plant").

SOME PLANTS OF THE SUB-KINGDOM OF BRYOPHYTA

In this sub-kingdom are the plants without roots or vessels; plants whose female organs are flask-shaped, and whose reproduction is characterized by alternation of generations; producers of gametophytes and of sporophytes. In this sub-kingdom we note specially:

THE CLASS OF MOSSES, which comprises plants having a stem that bears leaves:

● The maidenhair bryum, very common on walls and rocks. In dry weather, its leaves coil up in a spiral. The capsule is long and pendant.

● The polytrichums, e.g. common hair cap moss (*Polytrichum commune*). These are recognizable at a distance, with their upright sporo-phytes and their hairy calypteras shaped like candle extinguishers.

● The sphagnums (e.g. *Sphagnum palustre*) (photo M), commonly called peat mosses because they grow in boggy places and their decomposition produces peat. The stem bears lateral branches (1) covered with small leaves. Observed through the microscope, these leaves (photo N) are seen to be finely perforated. They are made up of files of greenish living cells, surrounding empty cells. It is due to the presence of these empty cells that the sphagnums owe their absorbent properties.

PLATE 18—MOSSES

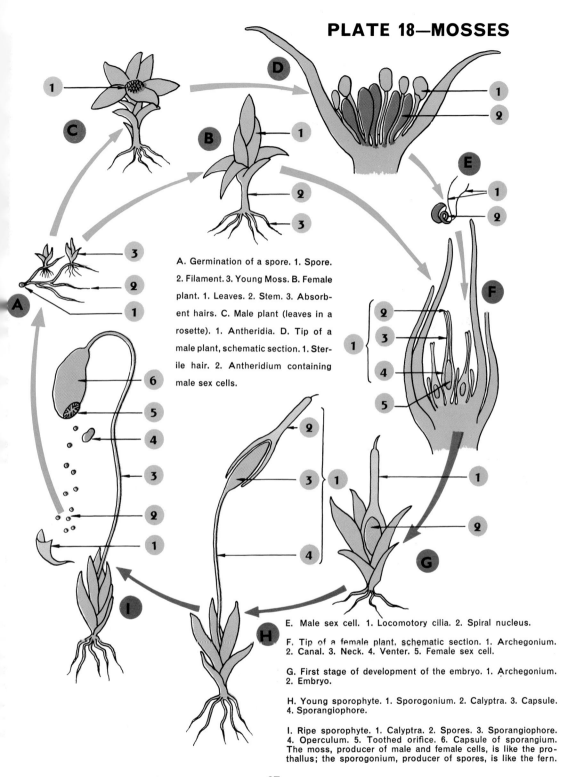

A. Germination of a spore. 1. Spore. 2. Filament. 3. Young Moss. B. Female plant. 1. Leaves. 2. Stem. 3. Absorbent hairs. C. Male plant (leaves in a rosette). 1. Antheridia. D. Tip of a male plant, schematic section. 1. Sterile hair. 2. Antheridium containing male sex cells.

E. Male sex cell. 1. Locomotory cilia. 2. Spiral nucleus.

F. Tip of a female plant, schematic section. 1. Archegonium. 2. Canal. 3. Neck. 4. Venter. 5. Female sex cell.

G. First stage of development of the embryo. 1. Archegonium. 2. Embryo.

H. Young sporophyte. 1. Sporogonium. 2. Calyptra. 3. Capsule. 4. Sporangiophore.

I. Ripe sporophyte. 1. Calyptra. 2. Spores. 3. Sporangiophore. 4. Operculum. 5. Toothed orifice. 6. Capsule of sporangium. The moss, producer of male and female cells, is like the prothallus; the sporogonium, producer of spores, is like the fern.

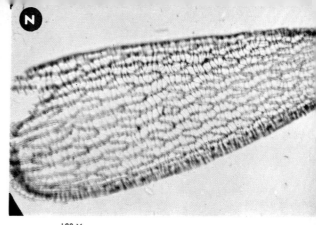

100 X

I X

THE CLASS OF HEPATICAS, the liverworts, to which the marchantia belongs (photos O, P, Q) a plant found at the foot of walls in damp places. It has the appearance of green laminae. But in spring and summer, small "umbrellas" develop on the laminae; some (photo P), deeply divided, bear sacs with female cells in the shape of bottles on their lower side: others (photo O), only lobed, bear sacs with male cells. On these laminae, small baskets also form (photo Q) which contain corpuscles used for vegetative reproduction.

I X

I X

X 1/2

SIMPLE FLOWERLESS PLANTS

Nearly all the plants studied in the first part of this book were notable for the beauty of their flowers of variegated shapes and shades. Compared with these, the plants we are going to study now may appear dull. In fact, this only appears so at first glance, as you will be able to see for yourself later.

The studies of these plants will be more delicate, and will often necessitate the use of a strong magnifying glass or even a microscope.

For example, photos D and E on page 93 depict diatoms, whose size does not exceed 200 microns (μ); they have a carapace with ornamentation of remarkable delicacy.

Apart from a few particular subjects requiring the use of strong magnifications and delicate techniques, observations mentioned here will be easy to undertake with an inexpensive microscope.

X 1/3

X 1/2

SEAWEED—AN ALGA

Seaweed is a common marine plant, which lives attached to rocks in the tidal zone. You do not have to be at the seaside to study it, as seaweed is often used for packing shellfish.

VEGETATIVE SYSTEM

Study a complete plant, such as common bladder wrack (*Fucus vesiculosus*) or rockweed (*Fucus edentatus*) which is shown in photo A. Fucus has the appearance of a branched thong; it is viscous, greenish, and is strongly attached to rocks by "hold-fast" anchors (hapteron) (1). This thong, crossed by a mid-rib (2), has small air-filled bladders here and there which act as floats (3).

A thin fragment of this plant studied through

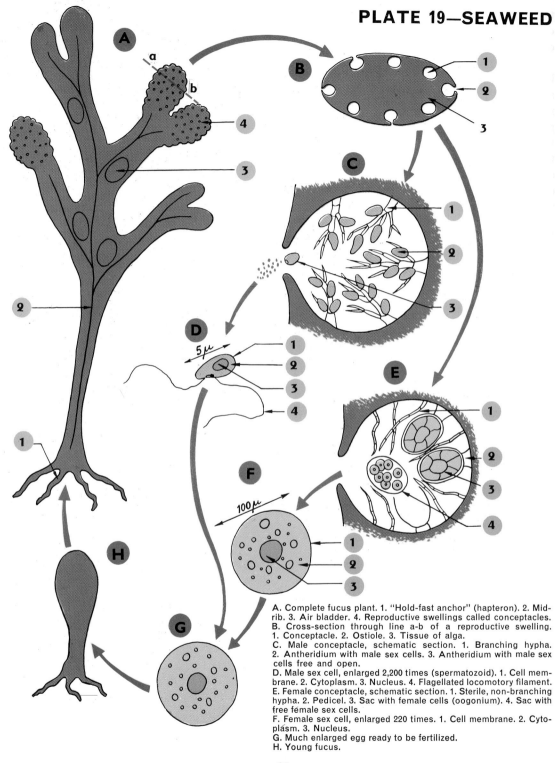

PLATE 19—SEAWEED

A. Complete fucus plant. 1. "Hold-fast anchor" (hapteron). 2. Mid-rib. 3. Air bladder. 4. Reproductive swellings called conceptacles.
B. Cross-section through line a-b of a reproductive swelling. 1. Conceptacle. 2. Ostiole. 3. Tissue of alga.
C. Male conceptacle, schematic section. 1. Branching hypha. 2. Antheridium with male sex cells. 3. Antheridium with male sex cells free and open.
D. Male sex cell, enlarged 2,200 times (spermatozoid). 1. Cell membrane. 2. Cytoplasm. 3. Nucleus. 4. Flagellated locomotory filament.
E. Female conceptacle, schematic section. 1. Sterile, non-branching hypha. 2. Pedicel. 3. Sac with female cells (oogonium). 4. Sac with free female sex cells.
F. Female sex cell, enlarged 220 times. 1. Cell membrane. 2. Cytoplásm. 3. Nucleus.
G. Much enlarged egg ready to be fertilized.
H. Young fucus.

the microscope shows that fucus is composed of a more or less thick entanglement of chains of cells.

The fucus is a plant whose vegetative system has no roots, stem or leaves. There is however an important difference between fucus and the fungi, discussed in the next chapter. Drop a piece of fucus in boiling water: it turns green while the water becomes slightly brown. Like the plants in the first section the fucus contains chlorophyll: fucus is an alga. Because the chlorophyll is masked by a brown pigment, soluble in hot water, the fucus is a brown alga.

LIFE OF THE PLANT

Fuci make their home along the shoreline at low tide, but are not in caves or where there is no light. This shows that fuci need not only water, but also light to live. You will learn later that chlorophyll-bearing green plants can, in light, use carbon dioxide and water to pro· duce chemically simple food molecules (sugars).

REPRODUCTION

On fuci gathered in winter (photo B), some ends are swollen and covered with small buds. If you squeeze these buds you will notice that a greenish jelly is exuded from some and an orange jelly from others. If these two jellies are mixed in a little sea water, a new fucus is produced.

If you examine the green jelly under the microscope (photo C), you can see that it contains small, spherical, immobile bodies (Plate 19, F). These are female sex cells which change into eggs.

The orange jelly contains a large number of much smaller male sex cells, which are motile, because of two locomotory filaments (Plate 22, D).

The swellings in which the reproductive cells form are the reproductive swellings (photo B, 1), and the stems that produce them are either male stems or female stems.

If you make a delicate incision in a male or female reproductive swelling (photo C) you will see small hollow spheres called conceptacles,

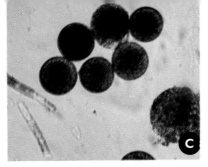

100 X

C

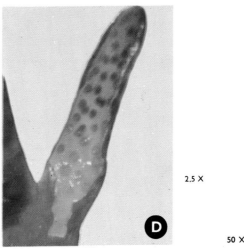

2,5 X

D

50 X

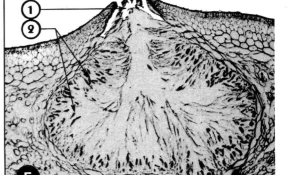

E

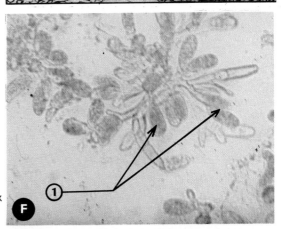

150 X

F

91

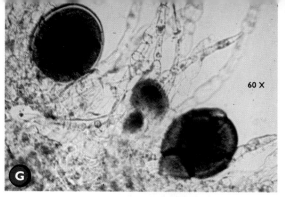

60 X

opening to the exterior through a small orifice, the ostiole (E, 1).

If the conceptacle is male (photo D) the sphere is full of branching hyphae (photo F) that bear orange swellings, in which the male cells are formed: these are the male cell sacs (antheridia) (F, 1).

If the conceptacle is female (photo G) the sphere is full of non-branching hyphae. The short hyphae bear large greenish masses (sacs), in the oogonia (corresponding to the arche-gonia in ferns and mosses), in which female cells develop.

NOTE: To study the contents of a conceptacle (male or female), crush it between two micro-scope slides in a drop of salt water.

The egg develops further when a male cell unites with it (fertilization), forming a new plant.

Conclusion

Fucus, whose vegetative system has no roots, stem, or leaves, is a plant containing chlorophyll masked by a brown substance. Fucus belongs to the sub-kingdom of Algae and to the division of brown Algae (*Phaeophyceae*).

SOME PLANTS OF THE SUB KINGDOM ALGAE

Included in this sub-kingdom are plants of very different appearance to the fucus, some-times living in the sea, sometimes in fresh water, sometimes in damp soil. But all are:
- Plants whose vegetative system has no roots, stem, or leaves.
- Plants possessing chlorophyll.

Grouping these plants according to color, there are:

Red Algae (*Rhodophyceae*)

In these, chlorophyll is masked by a red pigment. Most of these algae are marine. Their finely cut blades are often of great beauty, as you can see from photo A. Among these algae are:
- The corallines, whose vegetative system is impregnated with chalk: these are calcareous algae. There are numerous calcareous algae; the remains of some of these, collected as marl, find use as a soil conditioner for improving the soil.
- Irish moss (*Chondrus crispus*) from which a jelly is extracted, and used in preparing cer-tain culinary dishes.

Green Algae (*Chlorophyceae*)

These contain only chlorophyll. Examples are:

2 X

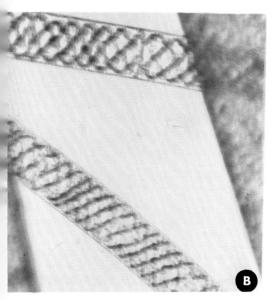

300 X

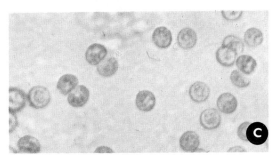

800 X

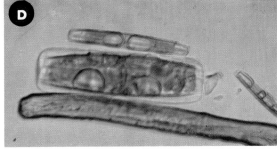

800 X

● Sea-lettuce (*Ulva lactuta*), having flat leaves: they may be eaten in salads.

● The spirogyrae (photo B), filamentous, fresh water algae, common in ponds and stagnant pools. Studied through a microscope (photo B) the spirogyrae appear formed of long chains of cells characterized by the presence of a spiral band, chloroplast, containing the chlorophyll.

On the surface of this chloroplast are areas called the pyrenoid bodies. When iodine solution is applied to a spirogyra cell, these pyrenoids turn blue-black, indicating that they store food as starch.

● The pleurococcus (photo C) is found on the bark of trees, on their least sunlit side, and has the appearance of a green powder. Through the microscope you can see that this powder is formed of small, detached spherical cells. Pleurococcus is a unicellular alga.

Brown Algae *(Phaeophyceae)*

Their chlorophyll is masked by a brown substance.

In addition to fucus, these include:

● The laminaria, which look like large straps, and sometimes grow to a length of about 16 feet.

● The diatoma (photo D). These are unicellular brown algae found in salt and fresh water. They often form brown deposits on the walls of aquariums.

By some means unknown to us, these algae can slowly move about.

The cell of the diatom is enclosed in a case impregnated with a very hard material—silica. Each case is formed of two valves which cover it like a box and lid. As you can see in photo E, this case has very beautiful ornamentation.

370 X   *Arachnoidiscus ehrenbergi*

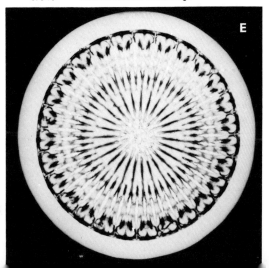

93

THE MUSHROOM—

A FUNGUS

VEGETATIVE SYSTEM

If you carefully uproot a cultivated mushroom (*Psalliota campestris*), you will be able to recognize:

AN UNDERGROUND PART, fragile, composed of white, tangled threads, rather like cotton-wool: this is the mycelium. A few fragments of this mycelium are visible (1) in photo A.

AN AERIAL PART (photo B) comprising: A white stem called the stipe (1), bearing a small collar or velum (2). A whitish cap (pileus) (4), under which radiate gills (lamellae) (3), which change from pink to brown according to the age of the mushroom.

If you examine a very thin fragment of the stem, cap or gills through a microscope, you will see that the aerial part is formed completely from a more or less thick network of colorless threads similar to those of the mycelium: the cultivated mushroom is a plant without chlorophyll.

Apart from this, the vegetative system differs very considerably from that of the green vascular plants: you will not recognize here any roots, stem or leaves.

NOTE: The name given to such a vegetative system is thallus.

I X

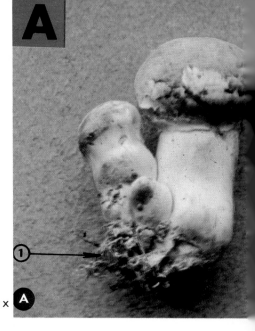

2 × **A**

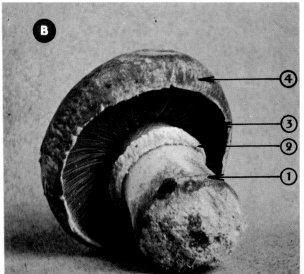

LIFE OF THE PLANT

Mushrooms can be gathered during late spring or early autumn, when we have warm, wet days. This indicates that these plants need warmth and humidity to develop. It is however in warm and humid cellars and caves that most of the edible mushrooms are cultivated. The fact that mushrooms can grow in shady places (forests) or dark places (cellars) shows that, unlike the green plants, they do not need light to live.

They grow on soils rich in humus; most of the edible mushrooms are cultivated on beds fertilized with manure. Mushrooms need as a source of their food decomposing organic matter. Thus the mushroom derives food nourishment as a saprophyte.

You will learn later that these last two facts are connected with the absence of chlorophyll.

REPRODUCTION

Set up the arrangement shown in photo C. You will collect on the cardboard (photo D) a brown powder whose design reproduces the appearance and pattern of the gills.

Examined through the microscope (photo E), this powder is found to be made up of small oval bodies called spores. Remove a gill of a mushroom, mount it dry between slides and

94

C X 1/2

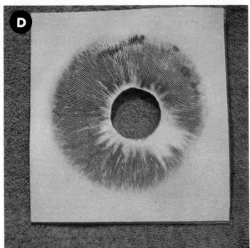

D X 1/2

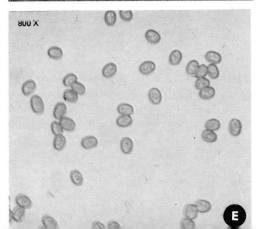

800 X

E

observe the edge through the microscope (photo F). It is apparent that the spores (1) are carried by the swollen end of certain filaments. These thread-like bearers of spores are called the basidia (2).

If they fall on the ground, the spores germinate. They produce numerous mycelial filaments which spread in all directions (photo G). As the oldest parts of the mycelium die, the younger parts produce aerial organs which in turn will produce spores. Often "toadstools" are arranged in circles called fairy rings. From nature, or with the help of the photos, you should be able to follow the growth of the aerial organs. At first, the mushroom has the appearance of a small ball, with the young mushroom enveloped in a very fine membrane called a universal veil. In some mushrooms, like the amanitae (Plate 20, D), this membrane is very thick and clearly visible.

If one of these balls is cut in two (photo J) you will be able to recognize a stem, a cap and gills. Earlier the universal veil split and disappeared. Stem and cap differentiate distinctly, but the gills (photo H) remain for a certain time hidden by a thick membrane, the secondary veil (1). In the course of growth the secondary veil splits in turn (photo I) but it remains attached to the stem and thus forms a ring.

The aerial organs, producers of spores, represent the fruiting body.

Conclusion

The cultivated mushroom is a flowerless plant whose vegetative system is a mycelium bearing aerial organs which produce spores.

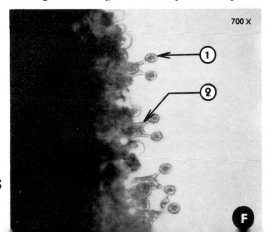

700 X

1

2

F

It is, furthermore, a plant without chlorophyll which draws the food it needs from decaying organic substances. The cultivated mushroom belongs to the sub-kingdom of Fungi.

SOME PLANTS OF THE SUB-KINGDOM OF FUNGI

Included in this sub-kingdom are more than 100,000 species, some of very different appearance to the cultivated mushroom but all are plants whose vegetative system has no roots, no stem and no leaves, and are plants without chlorophyll.

Without taking into consideration the characteristics on which classification is based, we can divide fungi into two large categories.

LARGER FUNGI

In this group are:

Edible Fungi

● The parasol mushroom (*Lepiota procera*). Its cap, covered with brown scales, bears white lamellae. It has a stem swollen at the base, a mobile ring, and its flesh is white. It grows on the edges of forests and sometimes in meadows.

● The chanterelle (*Cantharellus cibarius*) (photo K). The cap, at first ball-shaped in the young chanterelle, becomes hollow, forming a funnel with a sinuous border. Its flesh is yellow on the surface and white in depth. The chanterelle grows in woods from early summer on.

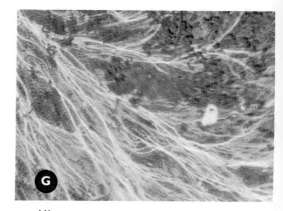

G

4 X

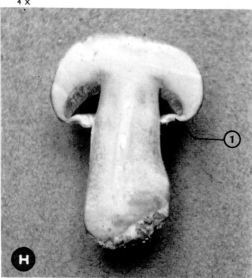

H

① I X

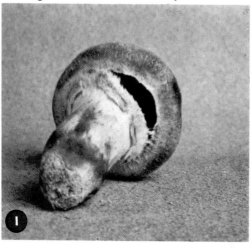

I

I X

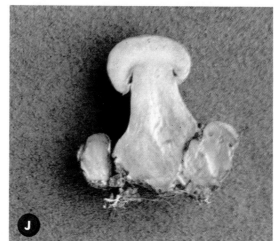

J

I X

● The saffron milk cap (*Lactarius deliciosus*). Its cap, often stained with green, is viscous. Its brittle flesh discharges an orange-red milky fluid. Common in pine forests, all these fungi are mushrooms with gills, like the cultivated mushrooms.

● The boletuses, such as the orange cap (*Boletus versipellis*). The cap reaches $3\frac{1}{8}$ inches in diameter; it varies between greenish-brown and dark brown and becomes viscous with age. With all the boletuses, the lamellae give way to tubes and the lower face of the cap appears pierced by a multitude of small holes called pores. The tubes are white but turn grey with age. The stem is tall and slim, wrinkled, and covered with blackish fibrillae. The flesh does not change color in the air. The boletus is found in leafy woods; only the young ones are edible.

● The hydne (*Hydnum repandum*). Its cap sometimes reaches 6 inches; it is curly, lobed, pale yellow or rosy white. Under the cap, there are no lamellae, no tubes, but very tightly packed prickles which bear spores. The white flesh yellows in the air. The hydne is picked in leafy woods.

● The jewelled puff-ball (*Lycoperdon germatum*) (photo L). In the young state, this is a globular mushroom, with white, firm, edible flesh. With age it turns purplish-brown and opens at the summit to free the spores.

● The morels (*Morchella esculenta*) (photo M). These are highly esteemed mushrooms

K

X 1/3

L

X 3/4

which generally appear in early spring. They are found in shady woods, pine woods, and clearings. The surface of the cap is covered with rugged hollows. If a fragment of the layer covering these cavities is lightly crushed between microscope slides, or better still, a thin section studied through the microscope after coloration with methylene blue, you can then see (photo N) that the depressions have threads, some of which, swollen and hollow, contain spores; these threads are spore sacs called asci (Ascomycetes): the morels are fungi with asci.

Non-Edible Mushrooms

● The rainbow conk (*Polyporus versicolor*) (photo S). This grows on rotten wood on tree trunks. In all polyporuses, the spores are

X 3/4

M

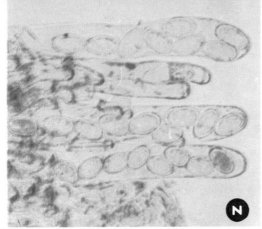

carried by tubes. The underpart of the cap, like that of the boletus, is pierced by numerous pores, hence the name.

Fatally Poisonous Mushrooms

● The death-cap or death angel (*Amanita*, sp.) (Plate 20 D), is responsible for 95 per cent of fatal poisonings. Like all the amanitae, this mushroom has a kind of cover, or volva (2) at the base of the stem, which represents the remains of the universal veil that enveloped the young mushroom. The inexperienced gatherer should therefore unearth mushrooms carefully to make sure they have no volva. This mushroom also has a ring and white lamellae. The death-cap appears in several forms (white, yellow, grey). In its yellow form it resembles the citrine amanita (*Amanita citrina*) which is harmless. Two other species, the spring amanita and the destroying angel (*A. verna*) are equally poisonous. They also have a volva, a ring and white lamellae. Every mushroom having, at one and the same time, a volva, a ring and white lamellae should be rejected for eating.

Dangerously Poisonous Mushrooms

● Fly-mushroom (*Amanita muscaria*) (photo O). This mushroom is easy to recognize with its red cap covered with white scales which are the remains of the universal veil. Its lamellae are white, while those of the true orange-milk agaric (which is edible) are yellow. The poisoning caused by this mushroom is serious but seldom fatal.

As a general rule, it should be remembered that there are many fungi which, without being fatal, can cause serious illnesses. Even edible mushrooms are indigestible if old. Remember too that no prescription exists for recognizing the good and bad fungi; the only way to identify them is to have a good knowledge of their botanical characteristics.

SMALL MUSHROOMS

Included in this group are:

Mildews

● The pin mould or mucor (photo P). This grows on fruits, jams, damp bread. If conditions are right, its fibrous thallus bristles with hairs,

98

PLATE 20—MUSHROOM

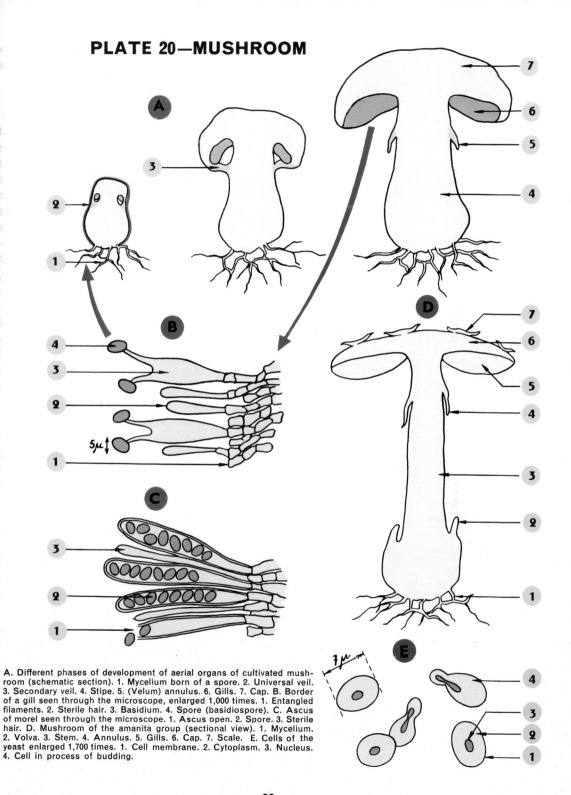

A. Different phases of development of aerial organs of cultivated mushroom (schematic section). 1. Mycelium born of a spore. 2. Universal veil. 3. Secondary veil. 4. Stipe. 5. (Velum) annulus. 6. Gills. 7. Cap. B. Border of a gill seen through the microscope, enlarged 1,000 times. 1. Entangled filaments. 2. Sterile hair. 3. Basidium. 4. Spore (basidiospore). C. Ascus of morel seen through the microscope. 1. Ascus open. 2. Spore. 3. Sterile hair. D. Mushroom of the amanita group (sectional view). 1. Mycelium. 2. Volva. 3. Stem. 4. Annulus. 5. Gills. 6. Cap. 7. Scale. E. Cells of the yeast enlarged 1,700 times. 1. Cell membrane. 2. Cytoplasm. 3. Nucleus. 4. Cell in process of budding.

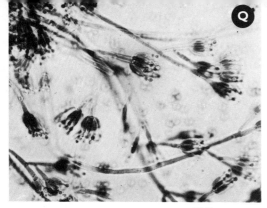

70 X

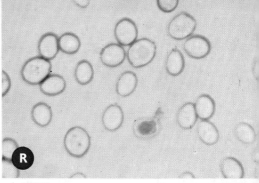

1500 X

X 1/2

soon ending in small black balls which liberate spores. These upright organs are called sporangia.

● Green mildew of the lemon (photo Q). This grows on damp bread and lemons. Its sporangia are branching filaments whose ends divide into a large number of spores. Because the sporangia look like pencils, the general name of penicillium is given to this mildew.

NOTE: It is a penicillium, namely *Penicillium notatum*, that provides penicillin.

Yeasts

Brewer's yeast (*Saccharomyces cerevisiae*) (photo R). Add a little water to a small particle of packaged fresh yeast and look at a drop of the liquid through the microscope. You will see a very large number of small oval globules. Each globule is composed of cytoplasm, surrounded by a fine cell membrane and cell wall. If you add methylene blue, you will see that in the cytoplasm there is a cavity filled with liquid: a vacuole. With highpower magnification and by using more complicated stains, you can discover that the cytoplasm contains a nucleus. The whole assembly of cytoplasm, nucleus, vacuole and cell membrane is called a cell. Yeast, which is made up of single cells, is a unicellular fungus.

In a sugar or molasses solution, the yeast cells multiply rapidly. You will see small swellings or buds form. The nucleus divides into two as does the cytoplasm, and each bud becomes a new cell. Yeast propagates by budding. You will discover that it is yeasts which are responsible for fermentation of sweet juices, such as the transformation of grape juice into wine. Without air, yeasts decompose sugars and change them into alcohol, while carbon dioxide is given off: this is alcoholic fermentation. This property is used in making bread and cakes—the carbon dioxide released raises the dough.

Parasitic Fungi

● Smut (*Ustilago tritici*). This fungus attacks wheat and its seeds are replaced by a powdery black mass of spores.

● Ergot (*Claviceps purpurea*). This fungus replaces the ovary of the flower by a black organ, curved and hard, causing a projection on the ear. The presence of a large quantity of ergot in rye flour can cause serious illnesses in people who eat rye bread. Yet, in small doses, extracts of ergot are used in medicine. Many fungi grow in this way as parasites on plants and cause large agricultural losses. They are similar to the ones that attack man and animals.

Cladonia   2 X

LICHENS

The wall lichen (*Xanthoria parietina*) is a very common plant which forms plaques, orange-yellow in dry weather, and greenish-yellow in rainy weather, on the bark of trees and on walls.

VEGETATIVE SYSTEM

The xanthoria (photo A) looks like a plate with scalloped edges whose surface is studded with small darker cuts. If it is dry, you will have some difficulty in separating this plate from its support, as it breaks up easily. To succeed, you must put the piece of bark that bears the xanthoria in water. You will then observe, in lifting the plant carefully, that it adheres to its support by some very short hyphae, the rhizoids.

The xanthoria is a plant without roots, stem or leaves. If you examine a vertical section through a magnifying glass (photo B), you will observe, top to bottom:

● A brown layer, lacking in other parts of the plant.

● A colorless layer.

● A green layer.

● A new colorless layer, thicker than the first, from which several hold-fast anchors run.

If you study through the microscope a thin section from this part (photo C), you will observe that the preceding colorless layers are formed of a dense entanglement of colorless filaments (3) like the mycelium of fungi. The upper layers (1) and lower layers (4), where

101

these filaments are most dense, are called the cortex.

In the green layer (2) and especially in the layer where the filaments are looser, you will observe small cells resembling unicellular algae (pleurococci).

It appears from these observations that the xanthoria is a plant formed by the union of an alga and a fungus. Such a plant is called a lichen. Various experiments have confirmed this. The alga and the fungus can be grown separately, and also, lichens can be reconstituted by putting together unicellular algae and the spores of certain fungi.

WAY OF LIFE

The fact that xanthoriae can develop in different environments, including stones on which no other plant can subsist, poses a problem about their nutrition.

A fungus cannot live in such an environment, because of the absence of carbon-rich matter. An alga cannot survive in an environment lacking humidity.

It therefore seems reasonable to conclude that there is an association of mutual benefit between alga and fungus. The fungus takes humidity to the alga by holding water in the mesh of its mycelium. The alga, because of its chlorophyll, can utilize the carbon contained in the carbon dioxide of the air and supply the fungus with its food. Note that algae are most abundant under the upper cortex, in which position they can receive the light they need.

REPRODUCTION

The surface of the xanthoria is often covered by a greenish powder. Through the microscope, this powder is seen to be formed of small masses

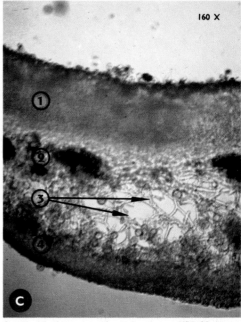

of several algae enveloped in mycelial filaments. Each one of these masses, liberated through tears in the blade, is capable of producing a new lichen. These masses therefore represent simple fragments of lichen, or slips: the xanthoria propagates through slips.

On the surface of the lichen, notice the cups. These are furnished with a brownish layer, clearly visible on photo B. Examine photo D, which shows this layer greatly magnified, and compare it with photo N on page 98. It too is composed of hyphae and sacs filled with spores, the asci. The cups of the xanthoria therefore represent the fruiting body of the fungus. These spores, germinating, produce mycelial filaments. In nature, if the filaments meet the right kind of alga, a new lichen is formed: the xanthoria is a fungus associated with an alga.

700 X

Conclusion

The xanthoria is a plant with no roots, no stem, no leaves, which results from the union of a fungus and an alga and which normally reproduces by slips: when a fungus is associated with an alga, it is an example of a symbiotic relationship (symbiosis).

X 1/2

E

Lichens with Simple or Branching "Stems"

● The usneas. The longbeard lichen (*U. longissma*) (photo E) which hangs beard-like from tree branches. The fruits look like small cups surrounded by long hairs.

● The cladonia or goblet lichen (*Cladonia pyxidata*) and red-crest lichen (*C. cristatella*). These lichens, when young, resemble blades. Later, they look like stems, more or less branching, and generally short. These stems often end in a trumpet (photo F) or in small clubs, as in the cladonia shown in the photo at the top of page 101, with its attractive red "fruits."

1 X

F

Lichens with Scalloped Leaves

● The parmelias which adhere to their support over their entire surface. They resemble the xanthoria and are generally grey or green.

Scab Lichens

● The lecanora which can only be collected along with its support.

Lichens in Upright or Pendant Thongs

● The evernia, one of which, the plum evernia (*E. prunastri*), very common in orchards, is recognizable from its thongs, hollowed into grooves, grey-green on one side, white on the other.

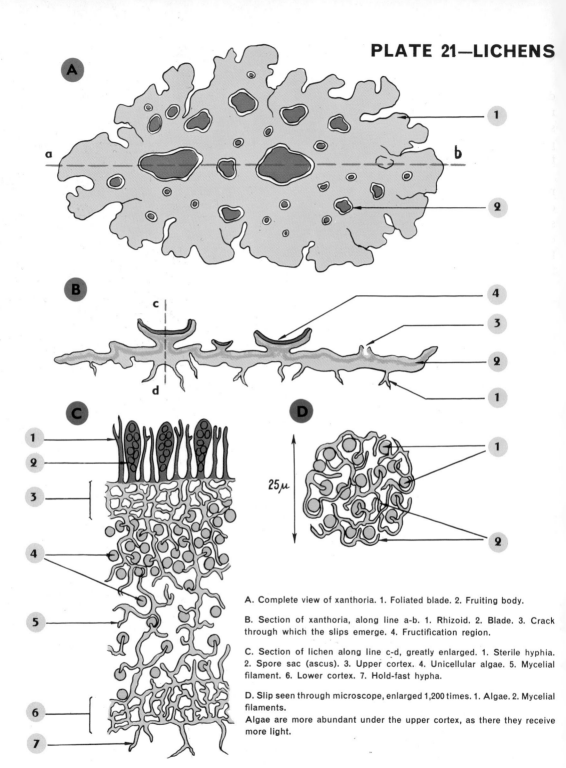

PLATE 21—LICHENS

A. Complete view of xanthoria. 1. Foliated blade. 2. Fruiting body.

B. Section of xanthoria, along line a-b. 1. Rhizoid. 2. Blade. 3. Crack through which the slips emerge. 4. Fructification region.

C. Section of lichen along line c-d, greatly enlarged. 1. Sterile hyphia. 2. Spore sac (ascus). 3. Upper cortex. 4. Unicellular algae. 5. Mycelial filament. 6. Lower cortex. 7. Hold-fast hypha.

D. Slip seen through microscope, enlarged 1,200 times. 1. Algae. 2. Mycelial filaments.

Algae are more abundant under the upper cortex, as there they receive more light.

CLASSIFICATION OF THE PLANTS STUDIED

The various plants studied so far are clearly distinguished from one another by a certain number of special characteristics. You have seen that it was possible to put together in one group plants having the same special characteristics.

In the same group, various characteristics make it possible to single out a certain number of sub-groups. For example, according to the shape of the flower, we have distinguished composites with tube-shaped flowers, with ligula-shaped flowers and with two kinds of flowers.

Many groups also have common characteristics. Besides the plants in the last two chapters, all other plants produce seeds containing the embryo of a new plant. In consequence, they are included in the sub-kingdom of plants with seeds or spermophytes.

Some, like the pine, have naked seeds, but all other plants have seeds enclosed in their fruit. The latter are placed together in the order of angiosperms (from two Greek words meaning "hidden" and "seed").

Among these, some are dicotyledonous such as the bean, while others such as the tulip are monocotyledonous.

Dicotyledons in turn can be divided into various sub-classes.

In turn, plants of the same sub-class can be divided into orders and split into sub-orders grouping a number of families.

It must not be supposed that classification was arranged at the very first in its present form. Old-time botanists, who knew nothing about male and female cells in the reproduction of plants, put them all together under the name of cryptogams, i.e., plants with hidden marriages. They thus opposed these plants to plants whose male and female organs they knew of, i.e., "plants with flowers," or phanerogams.

Later on, because the vegetative system of ferns is characterized by the presence of vessels, the group of cryptogams was divided into:

● The group of vascular cryptogams now called Pteridophytes.

● The group of cellular cryptogams, now called Bryophytes.

The following table summarizes the classification of the plants in this book.

GENERAL TRADITIONAL CLASSIFICATION OF THE PLANTS STUDIED

DISTINCTIVE CHARACTERISTICS			CLASS	SUB-PHYLUM		PHYLUM
PLANTS WITHOUT SEEDS	Non-vascular plants without roots, stems, or leaves		Many	Algae (Plants with chlorophyll)	Lichens	Simplest plants or THALLOPHYTES
			Many	Fungi (Plants without chlorophyll)		
	A stem— "leaves" or a lamina— no roots— no vessels	A stem, "leaves"	MOSSES (Musci)			BRYOPHYTES
		A stem, "leaves" or a lamina	LIVERWORTS (Hepaticae)			
	A stem, leaves, roots, vessels	Young leaves, crooked	FERNS (Filicineae)			PTERIDOPHYTES or Vascular Cryptogams
		Aerial stem, hollow, ribbed	HORSE TAILS (Equisetineae)			
		Slender stem, branching small leaves	LYCOPODS (Lycopodineae)			
PLANTS WITH SEEDS	A stem, leaves, roots, vessels	Naked seed	Several lateral seeds	CONIFERS	GYMNOSPERMS	SPERMOPHYTES or Phanerogams
			A terminal seed	YEW		
		Concealed seed	One cotyledon	MONOCOTYLEDONS	ANGIOSPERMS	
			Two cotyledons	DICOTYLEDONS		

PLATE 22—FLORAL DIAGRAMS

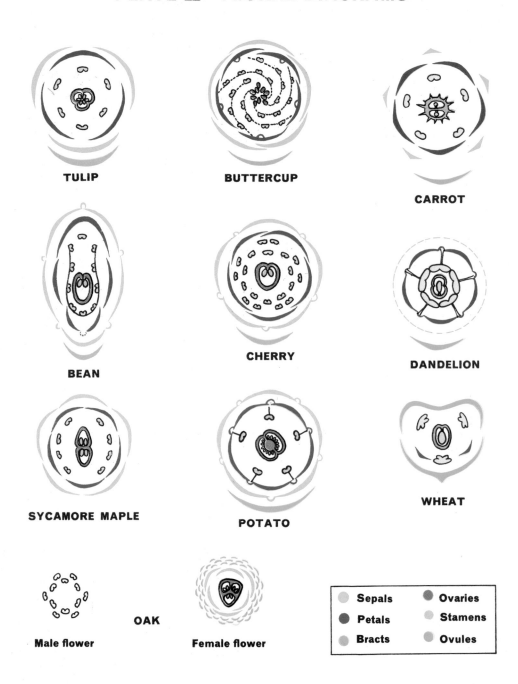

TULIP

BUTTERCUP

CARROT

BEAN

CHERRY

DANDELION

SYCAMORE MAPLE

POTATO

WHEAT

OAK

Male flower

Female flower

Sepals

Petals

Bracts

Ovaries

Stamens

Ovules

Aceraceae 22 A family of trees and shrubs, the maple family, having opposite leaves and small clustered flowers succeeded by fruits consisting of two united samaras.
Achene 18
Adventitious roots 13
Acorn 34
Air bladder 89
Alburnum 24
Algae 92 A primary division of plants without a true vascular system but with leaflike and stemlike parts, ranging in size from microscopic cells to giant 600-foot kelp.
Androecium 8
Angiosperm 56
Annual plant 12
Annual rings 26
Anther 8
Antheridium (-ia, *pl.*) 79
Apetalous 32
Araceae 52 A large family of plants, the arums, characterized by having flowers in a fleshy spike or spadix, and a leafy bract, the spathe.
Arborescent 26 To have the physical appearance, structure and growth pattern, especially branching, of a tree.
Archegonium (-ia, *pl.*) 79
Arums 50-53
Asci 97
Awn 49
Axillary buds 5
Bark 24
Basidia 95
Bean 5-12
Berry 30
Biennial plant 39
Bilateral symmetry 8
Blade 19 The expanded portion of a leaf.
Bracts 6
Branch 24
Bristle 85
Bryophyta 86 A group of plants consisting of the mosses and liverworts; characterized by the presence of a complex archegonia and a differentiation of stem and leaf.
Bud graft 77
Buds 26
Bulb 13
Burrs 35
Calyptra 85
Calyx 6
Cambium 77 A soft formative tissue giving rise to new tissue in the stems and roots of dicotyledons and gymnosperms and which throughout the life of the plant produces new phloem and xylem.
Capitulum 40
Capsule 14
Carapace 89 A siliceous shell.
Carpel 16
Carrot 36-39
Caryopsis 47
Catkins 32
Cherry 24-27
Chlorophyll 91 The green pigment found in chloroplasts; it is a necessary catalytic agent in photosynthesis.
Cleft graft 77
Coleoptile 47
Colorhiza 47
Compositae 41-44 A family of dicotyledonous plants, the largest in the plant kingdom; characterized by the absence of stipules and especially by the presence of a compound flower.
Conceptacles 91
Cone 55
Coniferae 56 A group of cone-bearing, generally evergreen, trees also known as the *pinales*; the largest order of gymnosperms.
Corolla 6
Corolla, irregular 40
Corallines 92
Cortex 36, 102 A plant storage tissue found in roots and stems.
Cotyledon 8
Creeping stems 74
Cremocarp 37
Cross-pollination 61
Culm 45

Cupressaceae 58 A widespread family of monoecious or dioecious conifers which bear small woody pollen cones with scales in pairs or threes and possessing opposite or whorled leaves.
Cupule (Cup) 32
Cuttings 76
Cypsela 41
Cytoplasm 100 The protoplasmic contents of the cell outside of the nucleus.
Dandelion 40-41
Deciduous 26
Dehiscence 73 The bursting open of a capsule or pod at maturity.
Diatoma 93
Dicotyledon 9
Dioecious Unisexual, with the two kinds of flowers on separate plants or in separate parts of the inflorescence.
Direct pollination 12, 60
Di-samara 21
Dispersal of fruits and seeds 68-73
Drupe 25
Dry fruits 70
Ears 49
Earthing-up 30
Edible fruits 70
Endocarp 25
Endosperm 47
Ensheathed leaf 17
Epicarp 25
"Eyes" 29
Fagaceae 35 A family of trees and shrubs, the beech family, including the most valuable hardwood timber trees, bearing alternate leaves, with male flowers borne in catkins and the female flowers solitary or in axillary clusters; with fruit borne either in a cupule (acorn) or a prickly receptacle.
Fecula 29
Ferns 78-82
Filament 8
Fleshy fruits 70
Floral formula 8
Flower 12
Flower buds 26
Flowering plant, structure of, 5
Fungi 96 A primary division of plants of the group Thallophyta; without chlorophyll, they are typically saprophytic, parasitic, or symbiotic.
Gametes 60
Gametophyte 79
Germination 9
Gills 94
Glumes 46
Grafting 77
Gramineae 47, 49 The family of grasses, one of the largest groups of flowering plants; monocotyledonous, they range from wheat, rye, and oats to rice, sugar cane and bamboo.
Gymnosperm 56
Gynoecium 8
Hapteron 89
Heart wood 24
Herbaceous 5
Hilum 8
Hooked fruits 69
Hybrid plants 63
Hypanthium 25
Hyphae 92 Threadlike elements of the mycelium of a fungus.
Hypocotyl 8
Indusium 78
Inflorescence 5
Internode 5
Involucel 37
Irish moss 92
Keel petal 6
Lamellae 94
Lamina 79
Laminaria 93
Layering 76
Leaves 5
Legume 8
Leguminosae 9 The legumes; a large group of dicotyledonous plants whose roots bear nodules containing nitrogen-fixing bacteria, considered variously as an order or family and distinguished by its fruit—called a pod.
Lemma 46

Lichens 101-104
Ligule 45   A thin appendage of a foliage leaf at the junction of blade and petiole.
Liliacae 16   A large family of monocotyledonous plants characterized by the regular perianth of separate segments, capsular fruit, and a bulbous stem base.
Lodicules 46
Margin 17   Outer edge of a leaf.
Maple 20-23
Mericarp 37   One of the two carpels forming a cremocarp, which split apart at maturity.
Mesocarp 25
Micropyle 8
Mid-rib 89
Monocotyledon 14
Monoecious   Plants having stamens and pistils in separate flowers on the same plant.
Mosses 83-88
Mushroom 94-100
Mycelium 94
Neck 79
Nectar 37
Nodes 5
Nut 34
Oak 32-35
Oogonia 92
Operculum 85
Ostiole 92
Ovary 8
Ovary, inferior 41
Ovules 8
Palea 46   In grasses, the upper bract which, with the lemma, encloses the flower.
Palmate 20
Pappus 40
Parchment wall 28
Parthenogenesis 67
Passive dispersal 69
Pedicel 6
Peduncle 6
Perennial plant 18
Perianth 12
Pericarp 7   The ripened and modified walls of the ovary.
Petiole 5
Photosynthesis 9   The process by which the chlorophyll, the green coloring matter or pigment of plants, transforms energy from the sun into stored chemical energy within a sugar molecule.
Phloem 24
Pileus 94
Piliferous layer 36
Pinaceae 54-58   A family of coniferous trees and shrubs known as the pine family, characterized by needle-shaped or scaly leaves and cones with flesh or woody scales.
Pine 54-56
Pinnae 78   Leaflets or primary divisions of a pinnate leaf.
Pips 28
Pistils 8
Pith 24
Pleurococcus 93
Plumule 9
Pod 8
Pollen 8
Pollination 12, 60-67
Potato 29-31
Prothallus 79
Protonema 86
Pteridophytes 81   A primary division of plants including the ferns, horse-tails and club mosses representing the highest division of flowerless plants. Characterized by being highly vascular plants, reproducing through an alternation of generation.
Raceme 6
Rachilla 48   A small or secondary rachis; an axis of a spikelet in grasses.
Rachis 48   The elongated axis of an inflorescence.
Radial symmetry 14
Radicle 8
Ranunculaceae 18   A large family of dicotyledonous plants composed of herbs and shrubs and commonly known as the buttercup family. Ranunculus,

familiarly known as buttercup or crow foot is a characteristic genus.
Receptacle 6
Resin 54
Rhizome 17
Root division 76
Roots 5
Rosaceae 26, 28   The rose family of trees, shrubs, and herbs possessing alternate leaves and flowers of regular shape. The fruits vary from dry to juicy and fleshy.
Runners 28 (See stolon)
Samara 21
Sap 24   The fluid contents or water solution of a plant, particularly that which circulates in the vascular tissue of woody plants, and which carries the raw materials of plant nutrition.
Sap wood 24
Saprophyte 94   Any organism living on dead or decaying organic matter.
Scape 40   Commonly, flower stalk; but actually referring to a peduncle arising at or beneath the surface of the ground.
Scion 77
Scutellum 47
Seaweed 89-92
Secondary veil 99
Self-dispersal 68
Self-pollination 12, 60
Sepal 6
Sheath 5
Simple flowerless plants 89-104
Solanaceae 30   A family of herbs, shrubs and trees with alternate leaves, showy flowers, a 2-celled ovary; includes many important food plants such as the potato, tomato and eggplant.
Sori 78
Spadix 51
Spathe 50
Spermatophyte 56
Spikelet 46
Spiral symmetry 18
Spirogyrae 93
Sporangium 79
Spore 79
Spore sac 79
Sporophyte 79
Spurs 26
Stamen 8, 12
Standard 6
Stem buds 26
Sterile flowers 42
Stigma 8
Stipe 94
Stipule 7   One of the pair of appendages borne at the base of the leaf in many plants.
Stock 77
Stolen 74
Style 8
Suckers 75
"Sulphur rain" 55
Symbiosis 103
Tap root 20   A primary root which grows vertically downward and bears small lateral roots that develop from the base upwards.
Tassels 49
Terminal bud 5
Testa 8
Tillers 47
Trunk 24
Tuber 29
Tulip 13
Umbel 25
Umbel, compound 37
Umbelliferae 39   A family of herbs and shrubs properly called the carrot family, characterized by the arrangement of the flowers in umbels and comprising among others parsley, parsnips and celery.
Umbellule 37
Universal veil 95
Vacuole 100
Vegetative propagation 74-77
Velum 94
Venter 79
Volva 98
Wheat 45-47
Wings 6
Wood (of tuberous root) 36
Xylem 24